Always Young and Restless

MELODY THOMAS SCOTT

with Dana L. Davis

★

ALWAYS YOUNG AND RESTLESS

★

My Life On and Off
America's #1 Daytime Drama

DIVERSION
BOOKS

For more information, email info@diversionbooks.com

Diversion Books
A division of Diversion Publishing Corp.
443 Park Avenue South, suite 1004
New York, NY 10016
www.diversionbooks.com

First Diversion Books edition, August 2020
Hardcover ISBN: 9781635766943
eBook ISBN: 9781635766899

Printed in The United States of America

3 5 7 9 10 8 6 4 2

Library of Congress cataloging-in-publication data is available on file.

To Edward, Jennifer, Alex and Elizabeth
With all the love my heart holds
XO

CONTENTS

CONTENTS

CONTENTS

ALWAYS YOUNG AND RESTLESS

FOREWORD

In this vividly engaging memoir, Melody Thomas Scott describes her adventures and triumphs as a child actor, as well as her horrifying experience of routine sexual abuse in ruthlessly careerist Hollywood. Fans of *The Young and the Restless*, where she has played Nikki Reed Newman for more than forty years, will find this turbulent backstory disturbing and fascinating.

"For me, Nikki's struggles symbolize perseverance and resilience," writes Melody. This tenacity is on striking display in Melody's account of her guerrilla warfare with her harshly dictatorial grandmother amid a chaotic home environment of unspeakable squalor. In these harrowing scenes of defiant resistance, we instantly recognize the early origin of Nikki Newman's valiant and indomitable spirit. Melody, with her Swedish immigrant ancestry, gave Nikki her own Viking hardiness and stoicism.

Daytime drama, which has alarmingly lost ground to talk shows and reality TV, descends from the great "women's pictures" of studio-era Hollywood, whose extravagant flights of heightened emotion paralleled those of Japanese kabuki and Italian grand opera. This baroque style has received new respect through the revival on

Turner Classic Movies of director Douglas Sirk's 1950s films, such as *Magnificent Obsession* and *Imitation of Life*. TCM has also highlighted Elizabeth Taylor's films from the same period, leading to long overdue tributes to her stunning power.

The classic soap opera style of deep emotion and dynamic theatricality is still flourishing in hit telenovelas throughout Central and South America. But on current US television, only four major soaps remain. Acting has also changed, with newer soap actors sometimes applying a cerebral methodology descending from the Group Theatre's progressive social realism of the 1930s. But ironically, despite their overt commercial framing, it is soaps that are more genuinely populist, as resoundingly demonstrated by their international mass appeal.

Melody Thomas Scott may be the last great practitioner of the soap genre—unless and until a new generation of young actors picks up the torch. Melody accepts and celebrates the unique protocols of her artistic process: as she frankly admits, soaps "exaggerate": "Our medium is often *not* based in reality." Soaps exist in their own universe of tangled relationships, simmering passions, and bruising conflicts. There are no final resolutions: the lead characters marry a dozen times, and even the dead can return from the grave!

In the glory days of Hollywood, the superstars did not disappear into their roles. On screen, they maintained a subtle channel of communication between their real selves and the audience, for whom they acted as proxies and surrogates in film after film. When Melody writes of craving a "life in front of the camera," she is defining the magic territory she inherited from her primary precursors, Elizabeth Taylor and Lana Turner, whose emotional purity, clarity, and simplicity were gifts that cannot be taught. As a bonus, Melody is also a deft comedienne, a master of priceless double takes.

With Eric Braeden's broodingly magnetic Victor Newman, Melody belongs to one of the most glamorous and charismatic super-couples in television history. Yet on camera, with her luminous, watchful gaze, she retains a heroic solitude, a legacy of her painful past. This book movingly chronicles a dual metamorphosis: the transformation of both a hard-working actor and her impish TV persona into the gracious, genial grande dame of today.

—Camille Paglia

PART I

★

THE
BEGINNING

1

I'M NOT ACTUALLY
STARTING AT THE BEGINNING

We'll begin with my fortieth anniversary party. (Because who doesn't love a good party?) I'd spent *forty* years playing Nikki Newman and a *grand* celebration was being planned. I should probably mention that no one on the show had ever officially celebrated forty years before I did. Doug Davidson, who plays Paul Williams, has been around for longer than I have; but, choosing to celebrate the milestone privately, his anniversary passed quietly.

Not mine. I'll always jump at a chance to celebrate something special. Spending forty years as a part of CBS's *The Young and the Restless* was indeed very special. And so I wanted this to be quite an event—which is exactly what it turned out to be.

I have heard, in roundabout ways, that some people who don't know me very well will come to one of my parties (I do like to throw them) and expect to see a scene out of the *Lifestyles of The Rich and Famous*. A glamorous event with only the upper echelon—actors, celebrities, that sort—in attendance. Perhaps they might find glamour, but they'll also find something quite normal. Regular people, my personal, non-show biz friends. Which makes me smile. Because normal is something I've been searching for my whole life.

The anniversary party was attended by so many of the people I love and adore. Sure, the actors and celebrities were there, too. But there were also former crew and cast members, make-up artists, hair stylists, old friends, people I hadn't seen in years. Each and every person in attendance had a connection both to *The Young and the Restless* and to me.

Like Diane Davis. You might not know who she is, but Diane was my longtime agent who sent me on the audition for Nikki back in 1979. And Bob Olive. Bob was my very first personal publicist, back before I even knew what a publicist did. Without him, it would've been a very different story—you probably wouldn't be holding this book right now and I certainly wouldn't be celebrating, at last, finding my normal.

Now don't think for a second that normal means boring. I believe in his speech that day, my beloved co-star Eric Braeden called me "obstreperous." (Confession: I had to look it up in the dictionary. It means "noisy and difficult to control." But I would have to respectfully disagree on both counts!) I think what my dear, cherished friend Eric was *trying* to call me, at least I hope, is unpredictable. Guilty as charged . . . I am, after all, the girl who stabbed Clint Eastwood with a needle—but I'll get more into that later.

I think perhaps people see me and think of Nikki. They see a fluffy blonde from Hollywood. They think I'm pampered. Spoiled. That I have an air of importance. A nose pointed toward the sky. But I think my longtime Southern buddy, Bob Caudle, said it best during his speech at the party. He told the story of how he took me fishing shortly after meeting my husband and me in North Carolina for a charity function. He didn't think I could catch a fish. Honestly, he probably thought I was more worried about breaking a nail. But on his boat, on lovely Lake Gaston, with a bottle of bourbon, I caught more fish than Bob did!

This is my normal. Traditional and grounded, sure. But *fun*. Normal for me is real connection. Normal for me is so much more than playing Nikki Newman or being a Hollywood actress.

The closing of my fortieth anniversary celebration would bring me to the microphone. Speeches aren't easy. And before you say, "But you're an actor!": know that it's not the same. When I'm in front of a camera I become someone else. But giving a speech, I'm myself, baring *my* soul. That's a horse of a very different color. I fretted about what I would say for weeks, because I knew I wanted to speak my truth. For the first time, *I* was ready to tell my story to my coworkers, my friends, my loved ones of so many years.

It was the story of how I found my way home. Crazy or not. Good or bad. Obstreperous? Not really . . . But unpredictable? Oh, *absolutely*. My fortieth anniversary party was a beautiful celebration that afforded me a platform to say thank you to all of those who have helped and blessed me along the way. But most importantly, it gave me the courage to finally open up and share the hurt, the pain, the near-death experiences (Oh yes, I've had them too). And now I am ready to share my story again.

With each and every one of you.

2

CHAIRWOMAN OF THE HOARD

I grew up in a house where the dust was so thick you could measure it—literally. I'd guess that it was a quarter of an inch or more. The kitchen floor would be sticky from spilled RC Cola and food debris, discolored from years of foot and paw traffic. The carpet was so filthy and embedded with animal hair that you could practically dig through it. Sure, we had a vacuum cleaner, but nobody ever used it. There was no order; furniture was strewn about and hundreds, perhaps thousands, of newspapers were stacked on the dining room floor. The table was overflowing with dirty dishes, dried food, and old, discarded packages.

Sometimes out of sheer disgust I might attempt to clear space in the kitchen. The roaches would scurry as I filled the sink with soapy water. The dining room table would be littered with so many dirty dishes, molded food, and trails of ants approaching from each and every direction that you could hardly see an inch of the tabletop. Besides, it wasn't as if anyone cared about my pitiful attempts to clean. The mess would simply pile up again, bigger and more impenetrable than before.

The filth of my childhood home is quite the contrast to the one in Beverly Hills I share now with my husband of thirty-five years, and an even bigger contrast to the home Nikki Newman lives in on Larkspur Trail where I *will* notice if even a tiny figurine is out of place. Now, back in the seventies, the term "compulsive hoarding" had not yet entered the popular lexicon. The home I lived in, with the roaches and the ants and the piles of trash and dirty clothes covering every square inch—it was simply called a big ol' mess.

So imagine my shame.

I knew other kids weren't living the way that we were. That caused me such pain. I longed for normalcy, but I knew we were anything but.

In the fall of 1956, my fifty-three-year-old grandmother was loading me up into our light-blue, Chevrolet Bel-Air sedan. Though she never allowed anyone else to sit behind the wheel, she certainly *should* have. Even now, I can remember her driving over curbs, barreling over mailboxes, crashing into things, trash cans . . . *animals*. She was a *terrible* driver, but I'll get more into that later. For now, she's loading me up for our daily drive to Santa Monica High School. My real mother had transferred from her former high school to avoid the embarrassment of anyone discovering that she was a sixteen-year-old mother—this *was* the fifties, after all. She was forced into marriage by my grandmother (to right the wrong of my conception, I suppose), and was living with my father somewhere near Los Angeles.

Every day my mother waited despondently during her school lunch hour for our arrival. I can only imagine her tapping her foot impatiently, her arms folded under her chest, her green eyes rolling in tempered frustration until she saw that Chevy in the distance and was finally able to join us on the outskirts of the schoolyard, where we would park on an obscure side street. She'd jump into the car to quickly and discreetly feed me, while my grandmother supervised.

I remember the disconnect. I can vividly recall the way she held me, as if I were a chore, as if some sort of parasite were attached to her nipple, sucking the very life from her. She did not want me. She did *not* love me. Don't ask me how I could understand and feel this at less than one year of age. I simply could.

This may be a good time to tell you that I have a rare gift/curse. A freakish memory, if you will. For instance, I clearly remember being a one-year-old. Two years of age? Yes. I remember that, too. I can remember events that happened when I was three as if they were yesterday. Ask me what scene I shot last week onstage at CBS and I may not be able to tell you. But ask me about my early childhood? I'll tell you anything you want to know.

Though my grandmother took on the duty of raising me, she was just as disconnected and quite obviously *discontented* with my existence as my mother was. Please don't imagine, even for a moment, that she was rocking me to sleep in a wooden chair on the porch, with a cool glass of lemonade at her side, while cookies baked in the oven. I don't think that there was ever any love involved, or cookie baking, for that matter.

Every morning I would be dressed in beautiful, expensive clothes. A photograph or two would be taken with our Kodak Duaflex and then I would be left unattended. Alone, I would spend hours gazing up into an empty room from my crib. I grew accustomed to being cast aside without a parent. In fact, by the time I was three years old, I went out of my way to avoid interactions with my grandmother altogether. If I should happen upon her, roaming about the house, I would freeze, terrified of a possible misstep, knowing that what typically followed an accidental encounter was yelling and screaming. I often bore witness to her fits of hysterical rage. I wasn't the only one who was afraid of her. But I was the youngest one.

I was raised by my grandmother but my grand*father* was in the house too—somewhere. You'd typically find him hiding in the attic, in a corner of the room where there was just enough space to fit the beautiful mahogany bed frame that held his old, dirty mattress, fitted with a sheet that never got washed. Most everyone called my grandfather Pop, except for me. I didn't call him anything, since we rarely spoke to one another. To me he was just "that guy." So I was raised by my grandmother with an occasional appearance from That Guy upstairs. Uncle Sven was living in the house, too. He was fourteen years older than me, so we were raised somewhat like brother and sister. I'd say my family was akin to a less adorable version of the Munsters. Remember poor, sweet Marilyn living in a house of freaks who think *she's* the hideous monster with all the problems? Well, I would've traded places with Marilyn in a heartbeat. Because in my grandmother's house there were strict rules to follow.

For one, I was forbidden to eat peanuts, because they would make me grow tall, and I was a child actor who needed to look younger than I really was.

Raw potatoes needed to be thrown backwards over my left shoulder to rid myself of calluses and warts.

Melted butter had to be drunk from a large spoon over the toilet to cure my colds and sore throats.

Showers were not allowed.

Bathing was only reserved for special interviews and auditions, and later, sexual favors for industry men.

Chewing bubble gum would give me cancer, so that was also forbidden.

Driving to Culver City would result in our untimely death, so if there were meetings in Culver City, we had to take a series of city buses that would take us hours and *hours*.

And though there were many piano teachers in the Larchmont area where we lived, *my* piano lessons needed to take place in Fontana, a small desert town an hour outside of Los Angeles. Because of my grandmother's fear of freeways, it would take us *twice* the usual time to make the lengthy trip, as she would deliberately limit her highway speed to a slow crawl.

In addition to her strange phobias and unexplainable life rules, I was required to keep my show business activities organized myself or else risk her wrath. She did purchase my clothes and costumes, but truly her only real job was to supervise me on sets and during classes, and drive us around town, while harping on "something."

Why can't you dance good? All the other kids dance good!

That was terrible singing!

Your voice is too high! You're always whining!

Do you know how unprofessional you are?!

You looked like an IDIOT out there!

Stop smiling so much! Your teeth are crooked!

You know that girl hates you? She HATES you!

She would also teeter-totter between overstated expressions of love and hate. She would buy me mounds of toys and expensive clothes to show love, but then she'd berate me with harsh words and criticisms, flying into a rage, personally blaming me for her state of unhappiness, and purposely ruining my own moments of personal happiness. It all served to keep me off balance, anxious, nervous, and angry. I never knew what she might say or do, or *why* she would say or do the things she did. I began resenting her overbearing presence in my life, as I was never sure which version of her I would be forced to deal with on a moment-to-moment basis.

Fantasy was my escape. I taught myself to be present only in body. In mind, I would travel far, far away to a place where I felt safe. There was a favorite fantasy of mine: a bathroom prison. Now, to most people, the thought of a prison might not seem too enticing. But for me, prison was the only space I could imagine that would ensure I could be kept locked away and protected from *her*.

In my fantasy, I would calmly count the tiles on the bathroom floor while I sat beside a bathtub filled with magical oranges. Magical, in that every time I ate one, another would take its place. Oranges were my favorite food and in my fantasy of solitude, they would be endless. My grandmother could scream at me until her tongue fell out. None of it could affect me. I was safe, counting tiles in a bathroom prison. Eating *all* the magical oranges I desired.

Where was my mother during all of this? At this point she'd divorced my father and given up on the responsibility of parenting completely. She took off to live a carefree, single life in another city. I often envisioned her, somewhere far away, dancing around in a circle on a busy street, happily tossing a blue and black winter cap into the sky, the *Mary Tyler Moore* theme blaring in the background, and wondered if she ever thought of me.

Happy and carefree, absentee mother aside, I was your typical bright, obedient child. True enough, I never received any hugs and kisses, or bubble baths at night followed by bedtime stories. In fact, my grandmother had an aversion to water. To her, bathing was *bad*. I kid you not. She considered it almost taboo, an activity to be *suspicious* of. One day, curiosity made me notice the shower head hidden behind our frosted, glass shower door for the first time and ask, "What's that?" as my grandmother shuffled by the bathroom.

"That's a shower and it's *not* to be used by you. Showers are not for girls. Girls don't shower."

"They don't?" I asked.

"They don't!" she snapped. "They're only for men, do you understand me? Don't ever let me see you touching it!"

So I never did.

Everything I knew and learned before school age, I pretty much figured out on my own. Even my pursuits in music began with my three-year-old self noticing there was a piano stuffed into a corner of the living room. One day, I opened the piano bench lid and found several beginner's instructional books, located middle C, and taught myself how to play.

I tried to keep my new ability a secret, fearful that my grandmother might disapprove and rage at me for toying with the expensive instrument. Surely, I wasn't supposed to be playing with something that was hers. But of course, a few months in, my grandmother did catch me. I stopped my tinkering, anticipating the hysterical screams that typically came with our encounters. But to my surprise, she was pleased. Delighted, in fact. *Another* seed was planted in her head. I was to start piano lessons in preparation to become a concert pianist. In time, though. Because the first seed planted in her mind regarding what was to happen with my life had already begun sprouting.

You see, my grandmother had Hollywood aspirations, and not having any talent did little to stop her from dreaming. Long before I was born, my family, Swedish immigrants, were living in upstate New York. A nationwide search from a major Hollywood studio was being conducted, looking for a new child star. Back then, it was common for studios to send talent scouts out in search of raw talent—not so anymore! Aunt Lillian, my grandmother and grandfather's firstborn, was chosen as the winner. The prize? A train trip across the country to Hollywood, culminating in the all-important screen test. My grandmother was over the moon.

However, after the trip and screen test, nothing happened. No major role in a movie or even a bit part ever materialized for Aunt Lillian. Still, my grandmother decided she didn't want to leave California. And without consulting anyone, she rented a house in Hollywood and moved into it. Afterwards, she called the rest of family back east, gave them the address, and told them where they'd all be living from now on. Clearly she had desperate dreams of making it *somehow* in Hollywood. Then I came along. The perfect answer to her prayers. Exactly what she had been waiting for.

* * *

"Hey! Get away from the TV!" my uncle screamed.

Uncle Sven had no friends, no girlfriend, and no social activities. Not that I knew of anyway. He was a rather ordinary seventeen-year-old. His brown hair was combed back and greasy from never being washed. He had an oval face, unassuming eyes, and a passive disposition. He didn't cause trouble. He listened and did exactly what my grandmother told him to do. When he wasn't at school, he could be found in the living room, his body sinking into his own couch impression, watching TV on the black Zenith that was the forefront of our home. It was constantly on, even if no one was in the room.

"Look at me!" I chimed to Uncle Sven as I flitted across the carpet, dancing and twirling, singing into my mock microphone, which, at the time, was the curved handle of the upright Hoover vacuum.

"Get outta the way!" he shouted. "I'm trying to watch the game!" He desperately wanted me to go away and play by myself the way I typically did.

"Watch me!" I sang happily, ignoring his pleas as I continued to dance, grateful for my audience of one. "Watch meeeee!" I laughed, happy to have a playmate, convincing myself that Uncle Sven should be happy, too, even if he was telling me to go away. I wanted so badly to be watched, adored, admired, *noticed*. Only it wasn't Uncle Sven who was watching me during these home performances. Though I never saw her observing me in the shadows, in retrospect, I know that she certainly must have been.

I suppose one could say that my grandmother literally pushed me into the world of show business, shortly after those innocent days of child play. It's true, she did, but I must admit, I was a willing participant. When we were driving around town for auditions and meetings, I felt normal. When we were out and about, seeing to appointments, head shots, classes, and piano lessons, my grand-mother put on a fantastic *show* of normalcy—she was certainly an actress herself. She was pleasant. Kind. Polite. I yearned for this version of her.

I really did.

3

SADLY . . . ME TOO

It was a sunny Tuesday afternoon, and not a cloud was visible across the entire sky. I sat near the window, lining up toys around our family dog, Suzie, a black miniature poodle, who was my only companion at the time.

"Okay, Suzie," I whispered quite seriously. "I'm Shirley Temple and you're mean ol' Uncle Ned tryin' to take me away from the airplane man who loves me." Suzie barked in reply and I placed a doll right beside her. "And this is Mrs. Higgins. She's real mean, too."

There was a great commotion coming from the kitchen. I paused in my play and turned to see my grandmother standing alone, holding the handset of our black, rotary desk phone to her ear, the brown, fabric-covered cord pulled as far as it would go. Her lips, which were typically formed into a deep scowl, began to curl up around the edges. *Smiling?*

She thanked whomever she was talking with, quickly placed the receiver back onto the base, and rushed to where Suzie and I were playing.

"You got the spot!" she announced excitedly. "You're *in* the Meglin Kiddies! You're in!"

At three years old, I had been a student of the Western Avenue Meglin studio for some time, but had not been selected to be a part of the Professional Group—as the Kiddies were called. But I keenly understood what an honor it was to be accepted as *the* youngest member into the elite performing troupe. Founded by Ethel Meglin in 1928, the Meglin Kiddies was the preeminent professional academy for Hollywood child actors in that it churned out child stars. Judy Garland had been a Meglin Kiddie; Shirley Temple, too. Studios recruited kids from the Meglin Kiddies all the time. And now I was one of them. A fact that made my grandmother . . . *smile*. She was *proud* of me. Okay, she didn't actually say, *Melody, I'm so proud of you.* In fact, she *never* spoke such a phrase. Still, I knew at that moment that she must have been proud, and so I smiled, too.

Sometime after joining Meglin's, my grandmother pushed me into more training. I gladly went along with it, thrilled to have found a way to earn her love. So in addition to my Meglin Kiddies obligations, I was introduced to the 3 Arts Studio, known for their onstage theatrical presentations. I worked hard to stand out and would consistently be featured in their high-profile productions. After the grown-up actors would perform an elaborate musical theater number, I'd come out, fully costumed, and do the exact same dances and sing the exact same songs. The audiences would hoot and holler—they *loved* it. It was harmless fun.

Another one of my childhood activities was the Hollywood Children's Theater. It was founded and run by a man in his eighties named Cosmo Morgan. The first Sunday of every month, Hollywood Children's Theater would put on a performance at the Trouper's Club. Today the Trouper's Club is long gone, having been torn down many years ago, but back in the sixties it was quite the hotspot. Located smack dab in the middle of Hollywood on La Brea Ave., it had a large theater that could seat 300, with a full bar in the back.

Cosmo's productions drew big audiences, too, but in order to be showcased, you had to take weekly, private lessons at his big, fancy apartment at Whitley Towers, just north of Hollywood Blvd. My private lessons started out once a week, but I soon became one of Cosmo's favorite girls, so my studies with him began occurring more frequently.

At four years old, I was a cute little thing. Big blue eyes, long dark hair that hung to my waist. (You thought that I was a natural blonde?) My grandmother would buy me these beautiful, *stunning*, brightly colored dresses. I must have looked like a real-life doll. She would take me, the living doll, all dressed up in my Florence Eiseman dresses, to the posh apartment of Mr. Cosmo Morgan. He and I would sit side by side on his purple velvet sofa, in his grand apartment, opposite an actual, full-size stage he had built inside the room—that's how *big* his apartment was. My grandmother stayed to supervise and would sit in a chair perpendicular to us.

Cosmo and I would practice scenes together. We'd work on crying and expressing emotions. I can't be too sure how it happened at first, but as time passed, eventually I ended up sitting on Cosmo's lap during these private sessions. Little girls of this era didn't often wear long pants, so of course, my legs were bare and my beautiful dress, which hung mid-thigh, would be raised so that my underwear (probably dirty) sat right on top of his lap. It didn't take long before his hands found their way onto my legs and up my dress. After that it was particularly easy for him, to move his fingers onto and into my private areas. Sometimes he might even remove a hand from inside me to pause and deeply inhale the aroma from his fingertips.

The first time that it happened, I looked at my grandmother as if to say, *do you see what's going on here? Help me!* I innately knew that it was wrong. I wanted to be helped. Saved. Protected. But she did nothing. She only watched silently as his hands and fingers had their way with me.

Under my grandmother's supervision, Cosmo's sexual abuse continued for quite some time. I eventually came to the great misunderstanding that this was my duty . . . my *service* to him. If the three of us would go somewhere together, my grandmother would drive, Cosmo would sit in the passenger seat, and I would sit on his lap. I thought of it as *the lap thing* . . . where Cosmo got to play and I was forced to be a willing participant.

In the car.

At his apartment.

You see, my grandmother was so ambitious for me (and her) to succeed, that anything that I had to do to *maybe* get ahead in the business was fair play. It didn't have to be a director or a producer, either. A grip, a boom operator, it didn't matter. In her naiveté, *any* man in showbiz was one who could help us.

Strangely, she did have her limits. There was an illusory line that she had drawn in her twisted mind. I do recall one time quite clearly, when Cosmo wanted to show me something in his kitchen. The kitchen was on the far side of his enormous, French-style apartment; you had to go through a series of hallways, twists, and turns in order to get to it.

"Let's just you and I move to the kitchen," he said commandingly, always with a twinkle in his eye.

Now Cosmo had quite an authoritative way about him, so when he spoke, people listened. "Yes, Sir," was my reply and I stood to follow him as ordered.

But my grandmother wasn't having it. She could snap her finger louder than any man I've ever met and the sound was like a bullet exploding straight through my brain. That snap meant that I had done something very wrong in her eyes that needed to be *fixed—pronto*. Wherever I was, whenever I heard it, I knew I'd better spin around and look at her immediately. So as he was leading me towards the kitchen, I heard the snap, and like Pavlov's dog I stopped and looked back. It was written all over her face. Sequestered in that back kitchen? *That* would not be happening.

We left early that day.

To add more humiliation to the sexual abuse I suffered at the hands of Cosmo Morgan, I was innocently becoming quite sexually aware, and at home, I would start trying things out on myself. There is a vivid memory that comes to mind. I was not yet five years old and had been touching myself in bed without knowing that my grandmother was hovering at the door watching and listening. She would wait for me to finish before she burst into the room in a spitting rage.

"Let me smell your hands!" Nostrils flared, she was standing over me, her breasts flapping about, barely held up by her standard cotton bra.

I denied any wrongdoing as I presented my hands to her and she smelled them like a trained bloodhound.

"LIAR!" she shrieked in a Joan Crawfordesque, no-wire-hangers rage. "Don't you EVER do that again! Do you hear me?! EVER!"

And with that, she stormed away.

As I grew older, the illusory line that my grandmother had drawn became less and less definable. The rules changed when she needed them to. Touching yourself? Completely taboo. Unthinkable. But trading sexual favors for industry men? *That* was perfectly fine.

4

AND SO, MY FELLOW
AMERICANS . . .

In November of 1963, while I was sitting at my desk in a second grade classroom at Van Ness Avenue Elementary, an announcement came through the intercom speakers. The message was short and direct: *all students and teachers must come out into the hallway immediately*.

We placed our pencils down and exchanged confused looks, but of course we did as we were told and filed out one by one into the hallway. Moments later, our adored-by-all principal, Mrs. Silk, appeared. Her heart-wrenching sobs signaled to us kids how very serious this situation must be. She moved carefully to the center of the hallway and delivered the news. President John F. Kennedy had been shot and killed—*assassinated*.

We were too young to truly understand what it meant to be assassinated, but by the looks on the faces of our teachers, it was clear that the president's death was a devastating event. Teachers were weeping in the hall, and it was more than my seven-year-old mind could take in. Everyone was sent home immediately.

The walk home was eerie. Cars were pulling over to the side of the road as the news on their radios must've rendered them unable to drive. Strangers on the street were sobbing and comforting one another. That walk really opened my eyes to the enormity of what had happened. My personal grief was beginning to sink in.

I finally made it to the house and pushed through our front door to find a most bizarre scene: my grandmother, grandfather, and Uncle Sven (who was now twenty-one), dancing, singing, and shouting with glee around the television—seemingly having a *party*.

"Damn Democrat!" my grandmother barked, dancing around the living room. "He deserved to die!"

"And Catholic to boot?! Damn right he deserved to die," my grandfather replied with a one-two step. "Fucking n----- lover!" And he raised his hands in victory. "Thank God he's dead!"

I couldn't believe it. The president was dead and they were *happy*? I had never, *ever* seen my family happy. Sure, we'd been on vacations during which we stopped to pose and smile for a photograph or two, but this was my first time seeing them express true joy.

I *had* grown somewhat accustomed to their strange fascination with murder and mayhem. They would often huddle around our shortwave radio, listening to real LAPD dispatchers. If something happened in our jurisdiction and was broadcast over the frequency, we would all pile into the car and fly right over to the address. If they were "lucky" enough to see a dead body being wheeled out, they would be *so* pleased. For them, a front row seat to a Broadway show would pale in comparison to watching a coroner push a corpse out of an apartment building.

Still, it deeply hurt my soul to watch them celebrating the death of anyone. Especially President *Kennedy*, who we were currently learning about in school. I believe it was the black and white image of Walter Cronkite on our TV screen, visibly shaken as he informed the country of our loss, that finally made me tiptoe away to my bedroom.

I didn't understand why I wasn't like them. I was just glad that I wasn't.

5

THE BLONDE HAIR STAYED

In the spring of 1964, I had an audition with casting director Owen McLean at 20th Century Fox.

"What's it for?" I remember asking, since my grandmother had brought me a change of clothes after picking me up from school and I was dressing in a gas station bathroom. I should mention that dressing in gas station bathrooms before auditions was pretty much the standard for me.

"Called *The Sound of Music*," she quickly replied. "It was on Broadway or somethin'. Now it's gonna be a movie."

I scratched my dirty head as she continued to babble on about the production. I was told that Julie Andrews and Christopher Plummer—not that either name meant a thing to us at the time— were already involved, and if I got the part we'd be flying on a plane to Australia (fans of the beloved film will quickly recognize my grandmother's error, as the feature was shot in *Austria*).

Australia or not, I was excited. I was always excited to go on auditions because of the normal moments they would gift me. And if I *got* the part, the normal would go on and on. I'd enjoy the crew, the on-set teachers, making new friends. It was like a dream world for me.

But mostly, it would give me *community*. Something I craved. Ever since I'd been a working kid, I always bonded with each member of the cast and crew. So much so that I would cry right on set on the last day of shooting. I hated losing the joy the on-set world gave to me.

I don't remember the subsequent callbacks, but I do remember reaching the screen test stage. For those not familiar with the process, getting to the screen test is a big deal. It essentially means the choices for the characters have been whittled down to a few actors to be presented to the studio in an on-set, filmed audition. I would be tested in scenes that required acting (in the governess's bedroom, scared of the thunder and lightning), dancing (various scenarios), and singing ("Do-Re-Mi"), which I sang in the key of C, as notes that I saved from that day reveal.

The day before the screen test, I was awakened with a declaration from my grandmother: "You will not be going to school today."

"Why not?" I replied in terror, as missing school meant answering questions from nosy friends, and I worked very hard at keeping the fact that I was a showbiz kid a secret.

"We'll be visiting a friend of mine."

I knew she had no friends, but said nothing. Later, we got into the car and took the erratic drive north to an old, broken-down beauty salon on Melrose Ave. I was seated in the lone chair.

"How would you like to be a blonde?" the owner of the salon asked me.

My eyes darted to my grandmother and she gave me a look that could A) kill me and B) clearly expressed I'd better answer yes.

The hairdresser waited patiently for my reply: "Um, I guess so."

A plastic cape was snapped around my neck and within a moment purple, stinky muck was being applied to every strand of hair on my head.

My hair extended well past my hips at that time, so the process took all day. When it was done, oh boy, was I blonde! I don't remember speaking or voicing an opinion, as I knew the only opinion that mattered was my grandmother's.

The next morning, I had an early call time at the studio. Driving through the gates of 20th Century Fox, I could think of nothing but *how am I gonna explain my blonde hair to the kids at school?*

My grandmother and I were directed to a soundstage where the Assistant Director checked us in and led me to the schoolroom. Most of the children present were the ones who ultimately got the part: Angela Cartwright, Brigitta; Kym Karath, Gretl; and Debbie Turner, who won the role of Marta, which I was testing for. Debbie and I were very similar. Except Debbie had dark brown hair. Exactly what I had just a day before. Now, I was a bleached bottle blonde—at eight.

I'll never know if my hair had anything to do with not getting the role. My grandmother simply never spoke of it again. And I dared not bring it up.

But the blonde hair stayed.

6

PSYCHO

I doubt my grandmother learned any sort of valuable industry lesson about changing your appearance the day before a screen test, because the new blonde tresses landed me my first role in a feature film. It was a big one, too. I would be playing the young version of Marnie in Alfred Hitchcock's 1964 thriller, *Marnie*, starring Tippi Hedren and Sean Connery.

At eight years old, I didn't know a thing about Hitchcock's legendary status. To me, he was simply another director. A very *scary* director. There was a scene in which my character gets slapped in the face in an alley. When it happened, a slight smile would creep onto my face, probably from surprise, as the young actress who slapped me made actual contact with my face. I remember Mr. Hitchcock's girth and the way he rose out of his chair and labored toward me, as he *never* barked directions from his director's chair.

"Do you smile when someone slaps you?" Mr. Hitchcock asked with his signature English monotone, followed by heavy breathing that seemed so labored it was as if it required a great deal of effort.

My mind tried to recall an organic moment of being slapped. But at this time, none of my grandmother's rages had ever escalated to physical violence. So I just said, "No, I guess not."

"Then do not smile," he replied with an irritated nod, and waddled back to his post beside the camera.

Days with Hitchcock were long and arduous, partly because, unlike any director I've ever worked with since, he would take excessive effort to literally *push* us into position.

"Do it like this," he would say sternly as he moved me to the correct spot. "Lift your arm like this!" And he would take my arm and haul it into the air. And instead of stating, *I want you to cross left*, he would literally push you into the blocking position, the physicality continuing take after take, until we'd all be allowed to go home for the day.

Still, Hitchcock and all, the experience was fascinating, and I found the people involved—whether they be crew, actors, or part of the production team—so utterly amusing, lighthearted, and . . . *fun*. A day at work was like going to Disneyland and this on-set experience quickly became my new normal. I wanted to live there and would've happily slept on the soundstage floor if I'd been allowed to.

Of course, it wasn't a perfect scenario as *she* was the guardian . . . and not of the guardian angel sort. My grandmother maintained a terrifying, disturbing energy that only I could truly perceive. I imagine it was difficult for her to watch me successfully existing outside of her control. I knew that as much as she loved living vicariously through me, she hated it, too. Because in those moments I was free. So she would work hard to reel me back in.

One particular work day, after finishing up a flashback sequence that took place in a drugstore with three other child actors, we watched the prop master breaking down the set, which had been completely constructed and built from scratch on a Universal soundstage. Naturally, we kids all gravitated to the large glass cases that held *candy*; the colorful, decadent kind that would need to be put into small, individual bags if purchased. When the prop master noticed us drooling over those glass cases, he told us we could take as much as we wanted. What did he care? They were probably going to toss it all in the garbage anyway. And since there were no bags, we grabbed as much candy as our small fingers could clench onto. I don't know where my grandmother was when this permission was given, but she suddenly appeared out of nowhere when she saw me leaving the set, chewing contentedly, still gripping my treats. Enraged, she grabbed my left ear, twisted it as hard as she could, and dragged me to the stage door. Once we were outside in an area of privacy, she let *loose*.

"What are you doing!? How dare you steal something off a set? Do you know how unprofessional that is!?"

I tried to interject, "But the propman said we could and . . ."

It was no use. She snatched the candy from my hands and left me standing in a dejected daze.

In retrospect, I believe my grandmother knew very well that I was *not* stealing candy. Right there, in plain sight, for all to see? No. She was giving me a tiny reminder that no amount of normalcy and happiness could ever upstage *her*.

She was in charge, and that was that.

Often, under her charge, the rash decisions my grandmother made would permanently bar me from what little carefree happiness I had managed to carve out.

One beautiful Southern California day, my best friend from school, Karen McClafferty, and I were sitting on the front steps of my house yakking about eight-year-old matters.

Where was the ice cream truck?

Do we have enough money for ice cream when the truck comes?

Have you heard Elvis Presley's new song?

I hear the circus is coming to town!

Then, from Karen: "How do you like your new teacher?"

We had been classmates since kindergarten, but I had recently been bumped up from second to fourth grade by my teachers. Unsurprisingly, this left me desperately missing all of my friends. Karen had been my *best* friend. Hearing from my grandmother and teachers that I had tested as gifted and would skip third grade was no consolation. For me, it was meaningless and unfair that I was now in a different classroom, studying different subjects, with classmates a full year older than me.

Karen and I tried to make up for the lack of "school time." Mind you, I wouldn't have been allowed to play with her at all if my grandmother hadn't deemed Karen's family as *"rich."* Her father was an OB/GYN and they lived in a *forty-two-thousand-dollar house.* This was heady information for an eight-year-old in 1964.

The McClaffertys lived in a beautiful Colonial-style house with a large swimming pool in its huge backyard. I was always begging to go over there to play—sometimes allowed, usually not. The reason? The McClaffertys were Catholic. My grandmother worried that if I spent too much time around them, I would one day return from a playdate newly converted. It was a serious concern of hers that cropped up more than it should have in the years to come. I guess the allure of their wealth made up for their crime of being Catholic.

Wearing shorts, we giggled nonsensically about nothing. With our bare feet dangling, Karen suddenly let out a shriek. "Oh my gosh, Melody, look at your toes!" A quick scan gave me no helpful information.

"What about them?"

"There's something wrong with them. Look!"

She eagerly pointed out the apparently appalling difference between her toes and mine.

Now, I had never really examined my toes, feet, or anything else that closely. I assumed whatever equipment I was born with was standard, shared by all humankind. Upon closer examination I discovered that yes, there was a difference between my best friend's toes and my own.

My second and third toe were connected. By flesh. Not all the way up to the tips, but enough to make me a freak of nature. Webbed toes.

This oddity escalated our conversation to volume levels high enough to prompt my grandmother to come out of the house, wanting to know what all the fuss was about. She revealed, in front of Karen, that I had inherited these webs from that "rat bastard, your father." The few times that I had actually seen my father did not include a body check.

Not only did my grandmother confirm that yes, something *was* wrong with my toes, but she tore into Karen for "making an issue of it." Karen was ordered to go home immediately. I went into our backyard, pretending to play with our cat, Nikki (yes, I know, fate!). As soon as my grandmother went back inside, I ran as fast as I could around the corner to Karen's house.

Neither her mother nor father were home, and their children had been left in the charge of Rayna, their housekeeper. Rayna's first language wasn't English, but that wasn't important—all she knew was that Karen had been provoked into hysterics by what my grandmother had said to her and that I, with the offensive toes, was part of it. Rayna knew enough English to tell me, "Go home."

I did, crying, hoping that my grandmother would call Karen's mother to clear the whole thing up. She did call later that evening. I only heard her side of the conversation, but her tone was hostile from "Hello." My grandmother's insensitivity and mean-spiritedness prevailed and by the end of the call, it was mutually decided that Karen and I would never play together again.

And we never did. I had lost my best friend. One might say that I lost her because of my toes, but that's not true. My toes were just a catalyst used by my grandmother to engage in her favorite pastime: spewing hostilities. I ached for her to be on my side, to be more like my friends' mothers, to love me.

But that person didn't exist. The abrupt loss of a friend over something so ridiculous never elicited any comfort from her. It was as if it had never happened.

Life went on. *Get ready for class. We leave in fifteen minutes.*

Years later, I asked my grandmother about my toes. She said that the attending doctor at my birth had mentioned the fairly common condition and suggested correcting them with a simple procedure right there in the hospital, when I was just minutes old. "Absolutely not!" Her suspicion of doctors and all things medical ran deep.

"I told him," she said, delighting in the drama, "that there was no way I would let them make a guinea pig out of you!"

My toes are still webbed.

Shortly after this event, my grandmother was backing the car down our driveway, late as usual in getting me to school. I was fussing with my notebook on my lap when our car's tires ran over something that made sort of a ka-plong sound. She looked at me quizzically and said, "What was that?"

I replied that I didn't know, focusing again on my schoolbooks. In an effort to determine *just what* that was, she put the car in gear and drove forward. Ka-plong, ka-plong, again. Now certain that *some damn kid* had left their toy in our driveway, she angrily got out of the car to gather the evidence. I got out too, already late for school. I started screaming hysterically when I discovered what was under our car: my dear poodle, Suzie, had somehow been let out of the house and found herself in the wrong place at the wrong time. I was so upset. As far as I was concerned, going to school was secondary to tending to Suzie, making sure she would be all right. My grand-mother wouldn't hear of it.

"Oh, no, young lady, you're going to school," as if she had caught me in an elaborate plot to play hooky.

"But I'm too upset to go to school," I cried.

"You're going and that's THAT." The subject was closed.

I entered my classroom still crying. My teacher immediately sat down with me to see what was wrong. As soon as I was able to get the words out I collapsed in heartache again. The school called my grandmother and asked her to come get me as I was too upset to stay at school. I don't know what she told them, but she refused.

As soon as she picked me up that afternoon, I asked her how Suzie was. She told me that Suzie was at the vet's office and she would be fine. It was the first time in my life that Suzie had ever *been* to the vet. No shots, medicine, or even grooming had ever been offered to sweet Suzie, as even animals had their own kind of *doctors*. That wasn't going to happen so long as my grandmother had breath in her.

For a while, I asked her how Suzie was doing every day; then every few days. Always the same answer: she was still at the vet, getting better. When I asked if I could go visit her, I was given a firm "no."

Time passed. According to my childhood diary—which I still have—two months passed, to be precise. On a Saturday afternoon, I was summoned to come in from the backyard and put my shoes on; we would be going on a car ride.

"Where are we going?"

"You'll know when we get there," she snarled.

I gleaned that it wouldn't be our usual driving duo this time when my grandfather and Sven got in the car, too. We got on the freeway and drove south for a long time, over an hour. Still a kid, I didn't pay much attention. I didn't even recognize that the park we ended up in was a cemetery. I had never been to a cemetery and didn't under-stand the implication. Our car finally parked at a curb; we got out and walked along a little path. The path led to a rather large grassy area with miniature American flags and plastic pinwheels snapping and clicking in the wind. In the middle of this plot, there was a large headstone with Suzie's picture carved into it. "To our dear Suzie, we will always love you," was on one of the more prominent placards, along with the date of her passing. It was the same date that she had been run over in our driveway. All of the "medical updates" had been a lie.

And that's how I found out about what had happened to my Suzie.

My eyes scanned up and down the program, finally spotting my name listed toward the bottom of the page: *Princess—Melody Thomas*.

I sighed and attempted to stretch out my toes in my custom-dyed, red tap shoes. Princess was really a fancy word for *loser*. I continued to skim the program to see who had been named the actual winner. There it was, displayed near the top in bold letters: *Queen— Alessia Ruffo*.

Only one girl could be crowned queen for the biannual *Junior Stars of America* beauty pageant and it was *always* Alessia Ruffo. I folded the bright yellow program in half and peeked around the stage curtain. There was Mr. Orville Rambo, gearing up to speak about Queen Alessia from the front row of the sparse "audience" at the Trouper's Club. I say "audience" because clearly the only spectators present at these pageants were the mothers of the girls involved.

Orville Rambo was the founder of another training troupe my grandmother had gotten me involved in. *The Junior Stars of America*. Mr. Rambo was a wealthy man, having made a killing in the stock market, and so every show and pageant put on by *Junior Stars* was personally funded by Rambo himself. He rented out the theaters, hired the crews, and essentially paid for everything, right down to our required costumes: specially tailored dresses so short that our requisite white-ruffled panties would show. Our hair was elaborately coiffed into Shirley Temple corkscrew curls, and we all wore bright red lipstick as per Mr. Rambo's preference.

The emcee would move carefully down the stage stairs to hand Mr. Rambo the microphone, which he would grab and hold tightly with his stumps. Worth noting at this point: Orville Rambo had no arms or legs. He sat in a wheelchair in order to get around and had a twenty-four-hour personal driver and caretaker.

Though he couldn't *personally* crown Alessia, he could drone on and on about her. "Congratulations to Alessia Ruffo, Queen of the *Junior Stars of America* beauty pageant!" His voice would echo in the nearly empty theater.

After a very light and unenthusiastic applause from the moms, he'd pause for dramatic effect, before continuing on about Alessia's merits . . . merits that had won her his personally funded gifts and accolades. Alessia couldn't play an instrument like I could. I was becoming quite adept on the piano. And she couldn't dance like me, either. I'd been training since I was three. She could get *through* a song, but I wouldn't go so far as to say she could sing. In fact, to be honest, Alessia Ruffo was completely with*out* talent.

So how did she always manage to score that giant crown, the gorgeous robe, and delightfully embroidered silk sash that officially named her the queen? Unofficially, the girl who won Queen was determined not by the talent on display at the pageant, but by what happened in the backseat of Mr. Rambo's car.

We were all "required" to have what I nicknamed *backseat sessions*. Mr. Rambo's personal driver would be at the wheel, and two or three of us at a time would be in the back of the car. All Orville Rambo desired was for us to take turns kissing him. My grandmother would be present for these sessions, standing outside watching or scrunched up in the back beside us. We were just little girls and we all wanted that crown. Since this was the only way to secure it, we kissed him—Max Factor red lipstick and all. I remember walking away after one of my backseat sessions and turning to wave bye-bye, only to see him sitting upright, wearing a rather pleased smirk, his face *covered* in red lip marks. I couldn't help but wonder how in the world, with no arms or hands, he'd wash it all off.

I never won that Queen crown, so I worried about Alessia and what she had to do to always earn it. I agonized about what she must have been forced to do to secure that crown time after time. She was an exotically beautiful girl. Dark waves of hair, dazzling green eyes, olive-toned skin. Her parents were Italian immigrants and like many showbiz parents, they were willing to allow their daughter to do whatever it took to get ahead. Years later, I heard that Alessia had run away, gotten into drugs, and became a goth, tattooed rebel. My first thought when I heard about her fate? Thank God she got away. I was happy for her.

I must admit, another reason why we all were willing participants in the sham of *Junior Stars* was that Mr. Rambo was our personal financier. He lavished us girls with gifts, tailored clothes, shoes, expensive lunches, and dinners at fancy restaurants. Alessia's tuition at a private school was financed by Rambo. The parents of *Junior Stars* got expensive gifts, too. My grandmother included. But I have to say she worked hard to earn them. She would often sneak into my bedroom late at night, long after I had fallen asleep, sit on my bed and call Rambo. They would gab and laugh on the phone until 4:00, 4:30 a.m. Annoyed at having been awakened, I would beg her to hang up or move to another phone. It was only when I was an adult that I realized why she never did. The phone in my room was the only one that wasn't within my grandfather's earshot.

I guess these "gifts" were an extra special "thank you" for allowing Rambo to have his way with their children's mouths.

* * *

At nine, I won a role in a stage version of *Summer and Smoke*. This was no sham, *Junior Stars*, freakshow circus. This was a Tennessee Williams production—a paid gig at a popular theater on Vine St. in Hollywood. In the stage production, there is a prologue portraying the two adult stars, John and Alma, as children. I was cast as the Young Alma. It was a lovely experience, with lovely people. But of course I was still a minor and my grandmother was still my official guardian. So there she would be, hiding in the wings, lurking in the shadows, eyeing me like a voracious hawk.

In my scene, Young Alma would kiss Young John. But in all the rehearsals, I kissed him on the cheek. During one of our final dress rehearsals, in full makeup and wardrobe, the director, whose name was Barry Baumgarten, called out, "I think the kiss should be on the lips. I'd like to see how that looks. Melody?"

"Yes, Sir?" I replied sweetly from the stage, in my high-pitched, baby-girl voice. Back then, I had a very high tone to my speaking voice that my grandmother *hated*. She would badger me to lower it and made me take voice classes so that I could learn to speak in a lower register.

"Can you kiss Steven on the lips this time? Would that be okay?" he asked.

My grandmother had trained me well. If a man in show business asks you to do something, you do it. So I called back, "Yes, Mr. Baumgarten."

It was just a peck on the lips. Innocent enough. Turns out Mr. Baumgarten didn't care for the change.

"Go back to the way it was before!" he called out from his place in the empty theater, pulling on the strands of his reddish-gray beard, as he continued to supervise the rehearsal.

All of this happened in a very rare instance when my grand-mother wasn't around. Who knows where she was. Getting fresh air? Sharpening her claws? I'll never know. She was simply away and missed this very pure moment of artistic expression.

No harm.

No foul.

Rehearsal continued and Steven, who was playing Young John, and I scurried off. We had become fast friends. We would frolic and play, running around with the stage hands, getting into all kinds of child-like mischief. At some point my grandmother returned to her post of supervising my every move and saw something that I didn't notice at the time; my bright lipstick was smeared all *over* Steven's lips.

Her public act of normalcy ended right at that moment. Without a word, she marched over to me, grabbed my ear and nearly twisted it off. She literally dragged me—still holding onto my ear—down the backstage stairs. I tried to tell her the director *told* me to kiss him on the lips. I begged and I pleaded, but it really didn't matter what I said. I had been "caught," and like so many times before, her rage would not be contained. Had my grandmother been present for the kiss, I'm sure it would have been fine. Obviously, I'd done much worse on her watch. But she wasn't present, and for whatever reason, a stage kiss on the lips was in her category of *promiscuous behavior*.

Looking back, I can honestly say that that incident was the moment where my tolerance and acceptance of my grandmother's behavior began to take a small turn; where my fantasy of escaping into a bathroom prison began to morph into something much more tangible. I was only nine years old, but as we drove away from the theater that day, her honking like a mad woman, weaving around cars and barreling through traffic, all the while hurling insults and criticisms at me, I knew that someday I would find a *real* way out.

7

(OOPS) I STABBED CLINT EASTWOOD

If the popular phrase that things get worse before they get better is true, then I suppose the fall of 1968 could've been perceived as rather exciting since Grandma's antics were spiraling out of control. Perhaps something better *was* on the horizon.

"Now you listen," my grandmother said conspiratorially the first day she dropped me off at John Burroughs Junior High. My eyes gazed in wonder at the sea of children marching contentedly into the large brick building. I couldn't help but worry that most of them might wonder what on Earth I was doing there. You see, the junior high school I was supposed to attend, with all my old friends, the school that was in my *actual* neighborhood where I'd lived my entire life . . . well, my grandmother had deemed that school unworthy. The public school *she'd* selected was an odd choice, not simply because it required a fake address for me to be admitted, but also because it would make me a complete outsider. The school's student body was ninety-five percent Jewish, three percent black, two percent other, and now one blonde-haired, blue-eyed me.

"These Jews might try to convert you," my grandmother hissed. "But don't you let them."

This might be a good place to mention that converting me would've proven impossible since we practiced no religion at all. I did go to a Presbyterian Sunday school, but only because my grandmother knew other child actors went there as well, and she wanted me to "stay in the loop." While I attended "worship," she'd sit in the parking lot in our car, reading the newspaper or trade magazines.

My worry, on the other hand—that the kids at my new school might not like me—proved to be a legitimate concern. I was bullied for being different. And when word got out that I was a child actor, things really got out of hand. I endured vicious verbal attacks and was continuously chased around the schoolyard by a particular group of girls who seemed intent on making my life a living hell. Some would randomly shout obscenities at me while others would threaten me with physical violence. The sad truth? I *longed* to fit in. To be friends with everyone. To blend. Look like them, talk like them. Thankfully, as the months in junior high dragged on, I did finally manage to nab myself a friend. Her name was Sandy Miller. But since no one was allowed into our home and I was banned from any and all afterschool activities, it always seemed a tough connection to maintain.

Still, school time was time away from *her*, and even better, time away from the hoard. Which, at this point, was a living, breathing organism—our very own ecosystem of layered filth and debris. I vividly remember the heaps of animal hair resting on top of our floors. Walls smeared with grime. Windows so unclean that sunlight could hardly pierce through the streaks and smears. Ripped and soiled upholstery with insides bursting out and onto the floor.

To add to my woes, I had begun menstruating. Now if you're imagining a scene out of a Kotex commercial with young me exclaiming, "gee thanks!" while Grandmother peacefully demonstrates the proper way to use a sanitary napkin, think again. Because I feared my grandmother's reaction, I hid the fact that I was bleeding by secretly purchasing Kotex pads at the Larchmont drug-store and hiding the used ones behind a bookcase in my closet. I suppose I decided I could do this forever. That those blood-soaked napkins would pile up infinitely and she'd never find out. However, one day the jig would be up. You see, back in my day, many kids in show business learned how to ride. Horses, that is. And if showbiz kids were doing it, of course my grandmother would insist that I do it, too. So one morning, before my scheduled riding lesson, I woke up with blood saturating my bed sheets. I was bleeding heavily and cramping so badly that I knew riding a horse would prove nearly impossible. Grandmother stormed into my bedroom while I pondered what to do.

She hollered, "Why aren't you dressed?!"

I'm not sure what came over me in that moment, but in an act of sheer defiance, I strode over to the bed and yanked the covers back, exposing the blood-stained sheets.

"I'm not going to riding lessons today," I declared.

I'm ashamed to admit, there was a part of me that imagined a true mother-daughter moment would follow. Where she would hold me tight, tuck a loose strand of hair behind my ear, and tell me everything would be all right. But of course she did and said nothing of the sort.

"Well," she finally stated, glaring at the sheets with disgust. "Things will never be the same again."

And they never were.

I can't tell you why this particular womanly rite of passage increased the chasm between us, but it did. I can only guess that this was an undeniable sign that I was growing up. No longer her little baby doll in her gilded cage. From this moment on, there would be an even greater disconnect. Whenever I found myself with basic needs—money for lunch, supplies for school, feminine supplies (something I would now be in constant need of)—she simply refused to provide them for me. This marked an even more abysmal era of home-life solitude.

It might seem like trying to manage my grandmother's rules, my troubled school life, the worsening hoard, and the sexual abuse I was continuing to endure should have overwhelmed and consumed a child my age. Or a child of any age for that matter. But I did have something special in my life. Something quite wonderful, in fact. Something normal. I was an actor. A *working* actor, to be more specific. While it had certainly started off as my grandmother's dream, a career very much forced upon me, it evolved, blossomed, and became *my* driving force in life. My escape. I could venture into a world where no one knew the secret pains of my life. I could escape into an environment where I got to be like other kids. I was much too young to understand whether or not I was truly talented. To me the marker for success was whether or not you were working. I worked. And if I wasn't working, I always came close to getting an important role.

I can remember being up for the role of Marcia Brady on *The Brady Bunch*. It actually came down to Maureen McCormick and me. *One* of the reasons she got the part over me is that she was taller. No joke! The creator, Sherwood Schwartz, wanted the kids to line up according to ascending age and height. There were pencil lines drawn on the casting director's office wall. I just didn't fit into the lineup. Still, Maureen and I looked so much alike we'd often audition together as twins. We were much too naïve and innocent to feel competitive toward one another, and there were plenty of roles to go around. It wasn't uncommon to lose out on a role and then get a phone call the very next day with an even better opportunity. There wasn't time to feel disappointed or left out in the cold. I'd be on the back lot of Columbia Studios, meeting with Bob Hope or chatting with some of Hollywood's most famous directors: John Frankenheimer, Ray Stark, and so many more. Or working on my favorite lot, Universal, shooting an episode of *Wagon Train*, *Ironside*, or whatever other fun came my way.

Speaking of *Wagon Train*, I had an eerie "reel"-life experience while filming my episode. Firstly, I played the daughter of Frances Reid—who went on to star on *Days of Our Lives*. Secondly . . . remember my earlier comparison of my home life to Marilyn's in *The Munsters*? Well, *The Munsters* filmed on the soundstage right next door to *Wagon Train*. Imagine our delight when Fred Gwynne, who played Herman Munster, visited our set. He did a bit of magic, told us riddles, and seemed to know just how to engage us kids. His show was a huge hit so it was a big deal that he was playing silly games on our stage. The shoes he wore as Herman had high platforms to alter his walk, making him appear as tall as Frankenstein. As if he wasn't already tall, those shoes truly made him monster-like! Even though we knew he was an actor, just like us, his sheer size along with his professional makeup seemed so real that we were hesitant to interact with him. It wasn't until Yvonne De Carlo, who played Lily Munster (looking so ghoulishly beautiful that we couldn't take our eyes off of her), joined him that my mind quickly shifted to remember the parallel of their make-believe life to my real one. Was my kindred spirit, Marilyn, going to join us next? She never did, but I do remember eating lunch in the Universal commissary a few tables over from Butch Patrick, who played Eddie Munster, and feeling sorry that he had to eat in full makeup—including those prosthetic ears—in front of everyone!

A life in front of the camera was the life I craved. Not because I wanted to be famous or loved and adored. It was just my normal. I'd even thumb through the trade papers that littered portions of the floor at our home, eager to see what projects were upcoming, what possible future meetings awaited me.

I'll never forget the day I saw an interesting article on the front page of *Variety*. It wrote of a nationwide search for young girls to star in *The Beguiled*, a gothic horror film starring Clint Eastwood, to be directed by Don Siegel. There was only one part left to cast. The part of Abigail, who was to be fourteen and chubby. Specifically. Now, I was neither fourteen nor chubby but somehow, I can't explain it—I didn't even have the promise of an audition—I simply knew the part was mine. I started to prepare. How? By eating. My favorite snack at this time (in preparation for a part I'd not even heard my grandmother speak a word of, mind you) was eating these hard, biscotti-like biscuits meant for teething babies, which my grandmother kept in our overstuffed pantry. "Zwiebacks." I decided they'd be perfect for the task at hand.

I'd slather thick globs of butter on top and stuff my face all day long. I also ate peanut butter and jelly, drank bottle after bottle of RC Cola, gobbled up liverwurst sandwiches with Wonder bread soaked in Miracle Whip, doughnuts, ice cream. If I could find it crammed somewhere in the pantry, and if it wasn't moldy (like much of our food was at the time), I'd eat it.

I got chubby. *Fast.* In fact, in only two weeks I'd piled twenty pounds onto my small frame. No lie. So it was no surprise to me when my childhood agent, Lola Moore, called one day soon after the weight pile-on. I had an audition. With Don Siegel himself. The movie? *The Beguiled.* The role? Why, Abigail, of course. The chubby fourteen-year-old. And if I didn't look big enough with twenty pounds of Zwieback cookie-and-butter weight on me, we went to Western Costume on Melrose, where I was fitted into a Civil War dress a good size too small with black lace up boots to match. I was nearly *bursting* out of the seams. I must've looked like quite the sight when I stepped into Don Siegel's bungalow on the Universal lot the next day. But after reading a few lines of dialogue, he simply gave me the part. Right on the spot. That very rarely happens. I wish I could say I was surprised. But remember.

I knew.

* * *

For those of you not familiar with Don Siegel, he's the man responsible for *Dirty Harry*, *Escape from Alcatraz*, *The Shootist*, *Invasion of the Body Snatchers*, and more, directing greats like Eastwood, Steve McQueen, Charles Bronson, and now me. Melody Thomas (no Scott yet; I was only thirteen, mind you). And for those of you not familiar with a young Clint Eastwood, let me offer you one word. *Heartthrob*.

The film was shot on location in Baton Rouge, Louisiana, and I was beside myself with glee. Though I was a minor and *she'd* be the one to accompany me, it thrilled me just the same. For I knew the normal that awaited me. Normal moments away from *her*. At this age I don't think I understood what it meant to hate someone. I simply considered my grandmother to be a mean, cruel, and vile woman. But I suppose in retrospect I did hate her.

Now it's worth mentioning that *The Beguiled* has since been remade (the 2017 film stars Nicole Kidman and Elle Fanning), but do yourself a favor and check out the 1971 original. Clint would greet us girls each day with a gentle kiss on the cheek. He was *such* a gentleman. And how did I repay him for his kindness? I stabbed him! I shall explain.

It was a normal day on set. Everyone was hard at work shooting an exterior scene that takes place after Eastwood's character has died, and all of us are preparing a Civil War-era coffin, which was essentially a canvas cloth that had to be sewn up over the corpse. There we all were, sitting on the ground in our respective positions, and there *I* was holding this long, extremely thick, authentic Civil War sewing needle. And there *Clint* was lying so still and peaceful. From the knee down, his right leg was resting in a hole to give the impression that it had been amputated (it was a gruesome movie). I'm not sure why the urge was so strong to jab him with the needle I was clutching with my chubby fingers. I tried to resist. But I did it anyway.

I stabbed Clint Eastwood.

With quite a thick needle.

In the foot.

As you can imagine, he jumped out of that hole *screaming*. Everybody was rushing and hurrying and panicking and wondering what on Earth had happened to poor, screaming Clint. There *I* sat. Of course nobody asked me what happened. I wouldn't have told anyway. I didn't confess my dastardly deed until decades later, at a luncheon at The Beverly Hilton honoring Eastwood. As a presenter, I decided it was the perfect opportunity to say, "So you remember that day when your leg was stuck in a hole and you thought you got bit by a spider?"

I think he's forgiven me. I hope so anyway.

There were older girls on set, too (much more mature than me and my jabbing fingers). Elizabeth Hartman, Jo Ann Harris, and Mae Mercer. There were three of us younger girls; myself, of course, plus Peggy Drier and Pamelyn Ferdin, who was quite the prolific child star at the time. We three would spend most of our time together, in the schoolroom, gabbing on set, and into the weekends. To add icing to my cake of normal—I'd gotten my very first invite to a sleepover. The film's cast and crew were all staying at the same "motor hotel," at which all the hotel room doors opened to the outdoors rather than an interior hallway. Us girls were laughing and telling jokes and secrets in Pam's hotel room. Talking about boys, I'm sure. At some point in the evening, I noticed fabric from my grandmother's dress pressed up against the window. I noticed the fabric stayed as the minutes turned into an hour or more. She was spying on us. On *me*. So I suppose I shouldn't have been too surprised when there was a knock at the door. Yet I was surprised. There she stood. Angry as usual, thin lips pursed into deep scowl. She announced that I would be returning to my room. No explanation. No reasoning. The sleepover ended at that moment. At least for me. I begged and pleaded but she was adamant. So with the heaviest heart, I made the sojourn back to my room. I was embarrassed, humiliated, and I cried the whole way, wondering why my life had to be spent with *her*.

In spite of my grandmother's presence there *were* tremendous moments of normalcy during my time in Louisiana. A balance, I suppose you could say. Working with the legendary Geraldine Page, who was as lovely as you might imagine, was a highlight. Working on a real plantation was incredible, too. I should mention that I've always had an affinity for the Civil War era, so the costumes, the location, the energy of the Deep South—it all suited me. I even enjoyed the set gossip from time to time. Perhaps you've read of a possible affair between Clint Eastwood and his young co-star during this time, Jo Ann Harris. She played Carol, who seduces Eastwood in the film. I certainly can't confirm or deny if she seduced him in real life. I can only confirm what I saw and heard during the shoot. Jo Ann was in and out of Eastwood's trailer. *Often.* We'd sometimes hear them fighting. Sometimes see her storm off. Sometimes see them make up, too. I was only thirteen but I imagined what was going on. *Everyone* imagined. But you know that popular saying—what happens in Vegas? I suppose it's the same way on a Hollywood set. It's a strange microcosm. A world all its own. Though the shrouded secrets do sometimes have a way of filtering out into the real world today—lucky for us, the internet didn't exist in 1970.

Still, in between the work and the gossip and the on-set shenanigans was *her*. Peeking around corners. Eyeing me. Waiting for her moment to pounce. Which inevitably always came. I can recall a cast dinner at a popular restaurant, Brennan's, in New Orleans. *Such* a good time. So much laughter and enjoyment. I'd noticed she'd excused herself from the table. I didn't think twice about it since one, I preferred her gone and two, I was having a wonderful time sans her evil glares and overall awkward and challenging personality. As we were all leaving the restaurant, there she stood, just outside the threshold. It was raining, so it added to the dramatics of her scene. Like something out of a horror film she was standing under an awning, tears streaming down her face.

In front of everyone, she said quite clearly: "I hope someday when you have children of your own they will treat you as badly as you have treated me."

Huh? What on Earth had *I* even done? My young self did not know. My older self, however, can look back in retrospect and see her conniving. Working overtime to rob me of well-earned happy moments. It was the one area in which she thrived. If making Melody Thomas's life a living hell was a sport, she was bound for Olympic gold.

Our time in Baton Rouge eventually ended and we all traveled back to L.A. to shoot the interiors on Stage 27 at Universal. We shot for about another month before the production came to an end. Wrapping up was always such a painful time for me. The cast, the crew—they became my family. Perhaps in some ways I feared returning to life with just *her*. Though even decades later in my work as an actor, I still find it hard to say goodbye to any production.

With the filming of *The Beguiled* over, I vividly remember pushing through the doors of John Burroughs Junior High. My grand return. I was so proud to share with all my teachers the wonderful grades I'd earned while on set with our fabulous studio teacher, Jean Seaman. Imagine my surprise when I discovered that my grandmother hadn't let the school know I was shooting a movie. In fact, since I'd left the school trim and blonde and came back fat, with ruddy red hair (production dyed it), they didn't even know who I was! Once they figured it out, they broke the news that I was considered a dropout. All the A's I'd worked so hard for while shooting in Louisiana were inadmissible.

I suppose it was a moot point as my junior high years had come to an end anyway. In just a couple of months I would be starting high school. Since the topic of *which* school I would be attending had never been discussed, I hoped and assumed I would be going to Fairfax High School with the rest of my friends from John Burroughs.

I was so wrong.

My grandmother had decided that a girls-only school would be the best choice. Even I could see through this plan; I was older now, and boys would certainly be coming into the picture. Meeting them at school, outside of her control, was simply not going to be a possibility. Without my knowledge she had been looking into one of the most prestigious private, all-girl schools in Southern California: The Marlborough School. I learned of this development out of the blue one morning when she informed me I had an appointment that day for an interview with the Admissions Committee. I would also have to pass an entrance exam.

There was very little time to mastermind a plan to thwart hers, but I was determined to succeed—and by succeed, I mean fail. When I walked into the admissions interview, I felt quite confident. Looking back, it was my very first attempt to go against *her*. I was officially preparing for a great rebellion.

"So Melody, tell us a bit about yourself," the charming admissions officer asked. I chewed and smacked my gum in reply. In fact, for the duration of the interview, I burped, gave non-answers, sat splayed in the chair, and acted like your typical teenaged *asshole*.

But even if they were willing to look past how awfully I acted in my interview, I made my admission into the school impossible: I purposely failed the entrance exam. To my delight, Marlborough wanted nothing to do with me.

But if this was a battle in a new war, my grandmother was up for the fight. She searched and searched until eventually she discovered a school that *would* accept me. Providence High School. A private, Catholic, all-girls school in Burbank, just across the street from Walt Disney Studios. Though I attempted the same antics that earned me Marlborough's rejection, Providence didn't seem to care how obnoxious I was. Shockingly, they accepted me. She had won the battle. There would be many more.

"Now you listen," she said conspiratorially the first day she dropped me off at Providence. "These Catholics might try and convert you. But don't you let them."

Where had I heard that before?

8

GIVE MY REGARDS TO
THE BROADWAY

It happens to the best of actors. A cooldown in one's career. A moment when you suddenly realize that your auditions are dwindling and your bookings have been reduced to none. A time when you must come to the realization that you are out of work. It's something many actors fear. *What if this is to be my last job? What if I never work again?* It's not like there's any real job security in Hollywood. So in truth, I wasn't at all surprised when it happened to me.

I was convinced the "cooldown" occurred because I was a bit of a sight. I still hadn't lost the weight that I had put on for *The Beguiled,* and my hair was partially colored a reddish brown with an inch or so of thick, dark roots. My grandmother decided my "fat legs" were to blame. Her words, not mine. Regardless . . . "fat" I stayed. Since I was convinced that I'd never work again anyway, high school seemed like the perfect platform to stage a *proper* rebellion. I was no longer choosing to be passive about the conditions I was being forced to live under. I wanted to upset her. Upstage her, if you will.

At Providence High School I worked overtime to get terrible grades. I didn't care about school, anyway. I would ditch class, forge connections with other "outcasts" at school, and break as many rules as I could manage. I cheated on tests, climbed out of windows, hid in offices, stole from the nuns . . . you get the gist. I was bad. Once, we hotwired Sister Juliana's car and took it to Bob's Big Boy for an early lunch. Not that we were even allowed to leave campus. I'm not sure if she ever even knew it was gone. Sometimes an antic might go too far and we would get caught. I'd fear the jig would be up. Surely the school would call my grandmother and tell her all the things I'd been up to and all the ways I wasn't succeeding. But strangely, the sisters would only call *me* into the office.

"Now we don't want to see you in here again, Melody," they'd say sternly. I would solemnly promise to try to do better. Then they'd dismiss me back to class.

Within the next week or two, I'd end right up in the principal's office again.

I felt untouchable. I didn't go to proms or dances or football games, but I really did enjoy my high school experience. It was my first taste of real freedom. And in retrospect, I liked going to a girls' school. I enjoyed wearing the uniforms. It helped me to fit in. And I actually enjoyed not having the pressure and distraction that boys would have created. But I never told *her* that.

One day a good school friend of mine, Marie, was applying for an afterschool job at a place called The Broadway. The Broadway was a very prestigious department store located at the famed corner of Hollywood and Vine. If you needed clothes or shoes or appliances, or anything in between, The Broadway was *the* place to go. She asked me to tag along.

"Sure, why not," I said with a shrug.

What did I care? Anything to avoid going *home* after school. But the store wanted to interview me as well. Imagine my shock when *I* was the one they offered the job to. I was working again!

Now most might think that going from Hollywood sets with professional makeup and wardrobe to roaming the aisles in a department store might feel like a fall from grace. But remember, for me, *normal* was my true pursuit. I was finally getting to experience being a regular teenaged girl. I was going to the beach with girlfriends, working a part-time job. Life was grand. At least from my perspective. To top it all off, working at The Broadway introduced me to Phillip.

I don't remember how I became aware of him, since Phillip worked up on the fifth floor in Major Appliances and I worked in Women's Shoes on the mezzanine, but somehow our paths crossed just the same. Remember that show, *All in the Family*? Remember Rob Reiner, who played the Meathead? Long, dark hair, mustache. That was what Phillip looked like! Sort of a blonde Meathead. Exactly my type, mind you. Even though I was still a sight—my long hair was an array of clashing colors, some parts ruddy red, some parts brown, all parts dirty, and I still was sporting my chubby frame— Phillip didn't seem to mind any of that. He liked me just the same.

I liked him, too.

Of course there was always the fear of *her*. A debilitating fear that my peace and normal would be ruined if she found out about my secret life of sanity. I worked hard to keep it from her. But perhaps I was careless. Maybe she saw the smiles on my face or noticed the way I'd take the phone into my room. She may have even listened at my bedroom door. I wouldn't put it past her. In truth, I don't know how she found out. I only know that she did.

As you can imagine, there was hell to pay.

I was visiting Phillip in the Major Appliances department on my break one particular evening. I was having a rather lovely time when suddenly she *appeared*. I swear it was almost as if the woman materialized out of thin air. Staring at me from between the blenders and hair dryers on display from the adjacent Housewares department, it made my blood run cold. She had an *oh poor me* look on her face, the identical expression to the day she stood dramatically under the awning in the rain in New Orleans. At the moment I noticed her, she marched her way toward me in a spitting *rage*. She knew. She knew everything. Well, at least she thought she did. But the truth was rarely important to her. She forged ahead with her onslaught.

"You whore!" she hissed. She continued with her tirade, standing there hollering and flapping her flabby arms about, calling me names. "Quit," she screeched. "I demand you quit this job right now. Or *else*."

Of course I did what any normal person would do when a mad woman is standing in a psychotic rage at their place of employment.

I called security.

"Oh, Mr. Hernandez?" I said sweetly into the phone as my grandmother raged a few feet away. "There is a woman here causing *such* a scene. Could you please come take care of this?"

Mr. Hernandez arrived soon after I hung up, guided her toward the exit and demanded she leave the premises. A few moments later, I was back in Major Appliances, doing my best to push the entire frightening incident out of my mind when guess who magically materialized again? Yep. Peeking out from around the electric skillets, standing in an aisle like she just escaped from a scary novel. I picked up the phone.

"Mr. Hernandez . . ." I sighed.

Once again, my grandmother was forced to leave my place of employment, but not before she gave me a stern warning: "I *am* going to see to it that you don't have this job beyond tomorrow."

I'm thinking, *oh yeah? Try it.* I sort of rolled my eyes and was relieved to see her removed. I was standing up to her! I was drunk with power.

Somehow I managed to completely avoid seeing her that evening and even the next morning before I left for the day. When I made it back to work, I got a message from the main employment office to please come upstairs. My heart was drumming up against my chest as I trudged up the stairs. *What now?* I remember thinking.

"We heard from your grandmother," one of the managers said very seriously as I stepped into the small office.

"Oh?" I said with an eye roll. I was still playing the role of the outcast. The girl who played by her own rules. The rebel.

"Mr. Hernandez threw her out of the store?"

I shrugged. "Yeah."

"She doesn't want you working here. She wants us to fire you."

My act of cool dissipated. I did *not* want to be fired. I loved my job. Loved my life away from her. "Please don't fire me," I pleaded. "Are you? Are you going to fire me?"

The manager shook his head and declared, "Absolutely not."

I was about to scream with excitement and relief, but he went on.

"You see, when you began here, your guardian signed a permission form. That form is legally binding. As long as we have that form, you *are* allowed to work here."

It was as if the air had been sucked from the room. Like my heart missed a few beats and left me breathless. I could only watch powerlessly as the manager searched through the files for a form I knew didn't exist. My eyes welled with tears.

For whatever reason, even though I was only sixteen when I was hired, an error was clearly made. My grandmother had never been asked to sign a permission form.

That day . . . that moment . . . I *did* have to quit my beloved job.

I hated her for it.

*   *   *

Perhaps the incident with my grandmother and Mr. Hernandez and that feeling of being drunk with power made me realize that I did actually have power. I wanted to exercise my right to use more of it.

I started with my acting money. I demanded it. Eventually she had no choice but to cough it up. *Some* of it, at least. I used some of what she gave me to purchase a car for $3,500, a brand-new Chevy Nova. And though I had to quit the job, much to her chagrin, I did not quit the boyfriend. In fact, Phillip and I were going stronger than ever though she *would* attempt to thwart my escapes from the house to go see him. One day she took my car and parked it behind an eight-foot tall, padlocked wooden gate in our backyard. Exasperated, I dug through the mess in our house, found a screwdriver, unscrewed the screws, and pushed the whole gate off its hinges. She saw what I was up to. How could she not? It took me several minutes to disable it. In turn, she took her giant beast of a car and blocked the driveway with it. Most of the homes in the Larchmont area were sort of on their own individual inclines. Many still are if you visit today. I drove as far down the incline as I could go and took off across the lawn until I made it to the neighbor's driveway and could manage a proper escape. I was a rebel *with* a cause.

I wish I could say this was one of few incidents but alas, we would go tit for tat pretty much every day. For weeks. Months. I remember being in a choir rehearsal at church, and after rehearsal ended I came out of the building to find that my car was gone. I was devastated to think that someone had stolen my beloved Chevy. Begrudgingly, I called the only person I knew to call.

"My car has been stolen," I reported to my grandmother on the pay phone.

"Well, no," she replied coolly. "Actually it hasn't been. *I* took it."

She had literally taken a taxi to the church and "stolen" my car with the spare set of keys.

"Why?" I cried.

She had no answer. It was a pretty dumb thing to do considering that *she* was the one who had to come and pick me up from choir rehearsal that day. In retrospect, I can only imagine that she could sense the war was turning in my favor. She knew it was only a matter of time before I would gain complete and total control over my life. I imagine it drove her mad and made her even more irrational, driving her to do nonsensical things like "stealing" my car.

9

SHAME ON YOU

A few months after having to quit my beloved job at the Broadway, I made a trip to the local DMV to take care of some paperwork and ended up standing in line with a teenaged boy. We started chatting, and discovered we had friends in common. It was an innocent enough encounter. We said our goodbyes, and he left before I did. When I stepped out of the building, there he was, waiting for me.

"Wanna come to my house and listen to some music?" he asked, leaning up against his motorcycle.

I should have declined the offer. After all, I did have a boyfriend at this point. Phillip and I were going stronger than ever. Yet I had this instilled conditioning. Behavior I learned from *her*, I suppose. I wanted to say no, but I hadn't yet learned how to. So I agreed, got in my car, and began to follow behind him.

This was a rather fascinating moment in my life because I remember it being the very first time I questioned my conditioning. Something didn't feel right. Sure, he was a man, but who says I should have to listen to him? If I had power over my grandmother, where else did my power lie?

It was raining that day and I stared through my windshield, watching as pedestrians scurried across crosswalks. I was mesmerized by the girls in their patent leather shoes, their clothes seeming brighter under the shroud of silver clouds. The parade of colorful umbrellas was almost magical. I longed to pull over and commiserate with these perfect strangers, walking so simply in the rain. I envied them. Their innocence. Their freedom. I could have joined them. The boy didn't have my phone number. He literally had no way of ever contacting me or seeing me again. And yet I still felt *bound*. I can explain it no other way but to say it was as if I *needed* to continue doing as I was told. Those moments when Cosmo's fingers were having their way with me and *she* would sit in agreement. It all was a part of my conditioning.

So all the way up Beachwood Canyon we went, under the iconic Hollywood sign, to his big house in the hills. We arrived safely in spite of the heavy rain, and we both stepped inside his home. It was a nice house. I began to relax a bit when I saw that his parents were there, watching television. I said hello and continued upstairs to his room, where he presented me with a glass of orange juice. I happily accepted.

"Thank you," I remember saying as I stood there talking to a giant parrot he had positioned in a corner. Perhaps a few seconds passed before I began to feel a bit odd. Something wasn't right. That thought was the last thing I remember before my memory took a jump. I don't know if I hit the floor or if he caught me before I did. All I know is that when I came to, I was naked on his bed and he was inside of me.

Yes, I was horrified. Shocked. Afraid. Saddened. I was being raped. I was too stunned to scream. When he was done, I gained enough strength to grab my clothes and stumble from the house to my car. Once I got home, I wanted only one thing. I longed for it. A bath. Even though in our house, baths were met with great suspicion. But desperate times, I suppose. I took the risk of incurring her wrath and drew one anyway. I sat in the warm water, my arms wrapped around my legs, my face wet with tears. In that moment I was all the terrible words she'd spoken to me over the years. A whore. A slut. *I should* be ashamed.

I was.

I had to tell someone, so I confessed to the only real friend I had at the time—Phillip. Phillip was a rare breed of gentleman. His reaction to me telling him that I drove to another boy's home? Kindness, understanding. He wasn't angry. Not with me, anyway. He grabbed his wallet and keys and insisted I get into his car.

"To go where?" I asked.

"The police station. You have to tell them what's happened to you," he pleaded. "You must."

In spite of my many protests, I soon found myself in the passenger's seat of Phillip's Volkswagen. I stood there in the police station with tears streaming down my chubby cheeks. Terror shot through me, imagining the words my grandmother would speak if she discovered what had happened. I didn't want to endure her rage. Her abuse. Now that I was older, she *would* attack me physically at times. A punch in the arm. A pull. A push.

I couldn't bear the thought, so I made up a name. I wasn't Melody Thomas that day, and I didn't live on Van Ness Avenue. Maybe I told the officer I lived on Wilshire. Perhaps I decided an address on Sunset would suffice. The finite details are fuzzy. What I do remember about that day, quite clearly, was that after Phillip and I were separated I had to speak by myself with *several* male police officers.

None of them believed me.

I was hauled from one room to the next. Shaking, crying, retelling my truth again and again. They *all* treated me with the same outright disgust and blatant disrespect. This was the seventies, after all, and women didn't have much power in a police station back then. At some point the universe decided to be kind and I was led to a female officer. *She* took the time to truly listen. She was attentive. Her countenance was troubled. At last, someone believed me.

She asked me if I could remember how to get to the rapist's house. I certainly could. In her unmarked police car, I rode shotgun, directing her to the exact house. She parked a few doors down from his family home and instructed me to wait in the car.

After about twenty minutes she returned, and said the boy was shaking in his boots. She had spoken with the parents, saw the huge parrot upstairs, and was able to confirm that everything was as I had said. On the drive back to the police station on Cole Avenue, she seemed hopeful that a case could be brought against him.

Instead of being happy to hear that, I fretted about what that would mean regarding my lies about my real name and address, but there was one question that terrified me more than anything. If my case was taken to court, would my grandmother find out?

I received a phone call from her a few days later. I'd given her Phillip's number in my efforts to keep my grandmother from finding out what had happened to me.

"This is Officer Williamson," she started.

In the end, there was nothing she or anyone else in the department could do about what happened to me. Though she believed that I was drugged when given the glass of orange juice, she said they could not prosecute. She explained that the DA had too many concerns with my story. Mainly, that I went to his house. Willingly.

"I'm so sorry," she said sincerely. "I really am."

I thanked her for her efforts and hung up the phone. It was over. My life could continue on. No longer would I be held captive by this nightmare. That was my hope anyway.

I turned eighteen shortly after the rape and I wanted some semblance of normal restored. So I marched right back over to The Broadway to see if I could get my old job back. I didn't need any guardian form to give me permission to work because I was now a legal adult. The Broadway was thrilled to have me return. I was putting my broken pieces back together. Trying, anyway. But weeks after the rape I discovered that I was pregnant.

I knew it wasn't Phillip's baby. It *couldn't* have been. That would have truly been an immaculate conception.

"Congratulations. It's a positive." The receptionist said cheerily on the other end of the line.

I was silent.

"Are you there?" she asked.

"Yes," I replied. I must've sounded as devastated as I felt because she added, "Is this not a happy moment?"

"I'm afraid it isn't."

"I see." The warmth and life was gone from her voice. She was cold now.

"Can I come back in?" I asked. "I need to see about . . . an alternative."

I was being vague but I knew she knew what I was talking about because she mumbled coldly, "We don't do that sort of thing here." And quickly hung up on me.

Thank goodness for Planned Parenthood. I did get the abortion. It was painful, embarrassing, and humiliating. The medical staff told me that I was doing a bad thing each step of the way. They criticized me, judged me openly. I remember it being so painful. I remember the utter humiliation.

I remember the shame.

But anything was worth enduring in order to not give my grandmother the ammunition that I was pregnant. I would have stopped at nothing to ensure that she never knew of it.

And she never did.

10

A STAR IS REBORN

Upper management imposed one hard and fast rule on me while I was working at The Broadway: never *ever* answer the phone in the stockroom. Maybe I wasn't so good on the phone? I didn't know. Didn't really care. I was thrilled to be back selling shoes and so I simply followed the rules and never answered it when it rang.

Well, almost never. One day, it started to ring and for reasons I can't quite articulate, I walked right over to it and lifted it off the handset. "Women's Shoes," I almost sang. "How may I help you?"

Incredibly, the call was for me! It was my childhood agent, Lola Moore. She was so chirpy and bubbly, as if only days had passed since we'd last spoken instead of actual *years*.

"Hi, Honey! I've got an interview for you."

"Um . . . ok?"

I wrote down the information without truly appreciating the bizarre happenstance that unfolded. The next day I went to the address in Beverly Hills to interview for a film.

I was still a sight. I hadn't lost the weight. My hair was an array of colors (two or three tones by this time), long, and dirty (I was still hardly bathing). But I showed up at the address Lola had given to me anyway because, why not? I got to the office and strangely I was the only actress there. The receptionist greeted me sweetly and guided me into the director's office. Turned out it was Kirk Douglas sitting behind a desk. *His* desk. I was in Kirk Douglas's office!

I sat across from him and he began to tell me about a new western he was directing and starring in entitled *Posse.*

"Oh, I love westerns," I remember saying. "I've done some, you know."

He nodded and took a long look at my mess of hair. "Do you know how to braid?" he finally asked.

I tugged on my long strands. "Sure."

He smiled. "Well, so can I."

The next thing I knew, he started braiding my hair. I know this sort of thing would never happen in today's culture but I can assure you, it was completely innocent. Kirk Douglas braided my hair. In retrospect, I imagine that he was hoping to get an idea of what I'd look like more "in character" because shortly after the braids were in place he said, "How would you like to join the cast of *Posse*?" (I know, this *never* happens . . . but this was the second time it happened to me!)

It was a whirlwind of activity after that. I was given details directly from his office. I learned we'd be in Tucson, Arizona, for an entire month. This meant I'd have to quit my beloved job at The Broadway again. It also meant something else. Something glorious.

"I will be traveling to Arizona to shoot a movie," I remember telling my grandmother, probably with a smug look on my face.

Her eyes were hopeful. I know she was waiting for me to say that I'd like her to accompany me. But I was eighteen now.

"I will be traveling alone."

She was hurt. I was glad to know it.

On that set in Tucson, alone, without my grandmother, I remembered where my heart was happiest. It was a tiny part that Kirk had gifted me. Nothing to even speak of really. But it didn't matter. I was sublimely happy. I understood now that being in front of the camera was something I simply had to do. For the rest of my life.

I had found my way back home.

11

THE GIANT TEDDY BEAR

S hortly after returning home from Tucson, I read in *Variety* that Don Siegel, the director of *The Beguiled*, was preparing to bring the novel *The Shootist* to the screen to star John Wayne. I immediately bought the book to see if it might have a part for me. It didn't seem to. But because it would be helmed by my former director, I couldn't walk away from the possibility of working with him yet again. (Mr. Siegel had already hired me to play the small part of the kidnapped girl in *Dirty Harry*, a year after we shot *The Beguiled*.)

So I formulated my plan. I had kept in touch with Mr. Siegel's longtime secretary, Ceil Burrows, since *The Beguiled* wrapped. I called her and asked if she could find a time in his busy schedule to meet with me for some career advice. I didn't mention *The Shootist* at all. She came through and the next day I was seated across from Mr. Siegel in his office. I told him that I was at a crossroads in my career and would very much like his opinion of what I should do: stay in the business or leave it entirely to focus on my piano.

He listened raptly and spent a few moments in thought. He inhaled, preparing to speak, and I knew that whatever he was about to say would determine with certainty my fate regarding his John Wayne project. Mr. Siegel then slowly pushed a few papers around on his desk, and . . .

"Well, Melody, I think you're a lovely actress. I could never advise you to leave the business in good conscience. As a matter of fact, I am about to shoot a new project called *The Shootist*."

"Oh, really?"

"Yes, it's a wonderful script and John Wayne has signed on to star."

"That's sounds exciting! What is it about?"

He gave me a brief synopsis of the western and added that all of the parts in the film would be "cameos." In the traditional sense, a cameo means hiring big-name stars to play even the smallest roles. When I heard that, my hopes sank. But then he thoughtfully continued, "There *is* a part, at the end of the story, that might be perfect for you."

Oh my gosh, things are suddenly looking up . . .

"I was about to give the part to another actress, but the more I think about it, the more I think that you should play the part."

And there it was. The *third* time that I was offered a role right there in the office!

Cut to me traveling to Carson City, Nevada, for on-location shooting of *The Shootist*. In those days, the studio's transportation department sent a car to the actors' homes to take them to the airport. I was riding contentedly in the back seat as we headed to Burbank Airport in L.A. But then we seemed to go off-route, heading in the wrong direction. I asked the driver if there was a problem. He told me that no, there's no problem, we were just going to make a quick stop on the way.

The quick stop turned out to be a veterinarian's office, from which we were to pick up Lauren Bacall's dog. One of the many stars of the film, she was already on location in Carson City and missing her precious King Charles Spaniel.

Upon arriving at the airport, our driver walked with me to the check-in counter. Having already checked myself in, I wasn't paying too much attention to his conversation with the airline rep. But their voices started to escalate. What I could make out was something to do with Lauren Bacall's dog. The airline wanted to transport the dog in a crate in baggage. Our driver was adamantly against that plan.

"Do you understand that this is *Lauren Bacall's dog? He does not travel in a crate!* We've already secured a seat in the passenger's cabin for him, so whatever you need to do to ensure that, you'd better do it pretty quickly."

The airline rep was suddenly on board (pun intended). Her only remaining question was who will be traveling with Miss Bacall's dog.

The driver then turned to *me*: "You'd be okay with that, wouldn't you, Miss Thomas?"

"Um . . . sure."

The next thing I knew, I was sitting in my first-class seat with Blenheim (yes, he had been named after the English palace) in the first-class seat next to me. I had been given special food for him, which looked suspiciously like bits of steak. He sat regally in his large seat, seemingly at home in his luxurious surroundings.

After the short flight to Carson City, a driver picked Blenheim and me up from the airport and drove directly to the location set, where Miss Bacall was anxiously awaiting her best friend's arrival. Our car came to a stop about one hundred yards from her outstretched arms. Blenheim heard her call and ran as fast as a dog can run to his mistress. Any reunion involving a dog is always heartwarming!

I didn't meet John Wayne until the next day when I shot my scene with him. An assistant director led me to Mr. Wayne's trailer for the introduction. He appeared in the doorway, bigger than life. As he walked down the steps to shake my hand, I was in awe of what a presence he was. So tall, the epitome of strength; it was hard to imagine that he was suffering from late-stage cancer. But, of course, he was, and the entire company knew it. I remember noticing some sort of copper bracelet on his wrist when his bear paw of a hand shook mine. A magical moment, colored by reality.

While we were shooting, he was nothing but charming, easygoing, and, well, so John Wayne! He really knew how to be a movie star. I feel so fortunate to have worked with him. *The Shootist* would indeed be his last film.

Shortly after I completed filming, I was speaking on the phone to Mr. Siegel's secretary, Ceil. She finally told me what she *couldn't* tell me earlier.

"Melody, do you know who was going to play your part before you had that meeting with Mr. Siegel that day?"

"No, who?"

"Goldie Hawn."

I couldn't believe it. Goldie Hawn had become the world's darling from her first TV series, *Laugh-In*, before she became the major film star she then was. She had already won an Oscar for *Cactus Flower.* I was certainly no acceptable substitute for Goldie Hawn. But somehow, Mr. Siegel and fate had stepped into my orbit yet again.

Many years later, a camera crew from Japan interviewed me in my dressing room at CBS. They told my publicist, Frank Tobin, that they wanted to focus on *The Shootist*. This was an unusual but sentimental request for me, so I agreed.

When they arrived, I noticed that they seemed quite nervous; I couldn't understand why, but it became evident as the interview began. I'll give my readers the information I didn't yet know as I sat in my dressing room that day: John Wayne, the epitome of Americana, has a *huge* following in Japan. Today. Forty years after his passing. Beyond hero status!

As we began the interview, the crew began visibly shaking and wiping the sweat from their brows. My interviewer, the only one of the group who spoke English, asked me very specific questions through his increasingly dry mouth. I offered water and tried my best to be professional. But their intensity only increased.

As we wrapped up, the interviewer politely asked if he could touch my arm. I darted a quick look to Frank, who gave me his go-ahead with the silent shorthand only I could perceive. I said, "Sure," and as his hand lingered, tears started falling from his eyes. He immediately apologized, explaining that he had been overcome with emotion speaking to the "last actress to appear on film, with John Wayne, ever!"

This calculation was based on the fact that after his scene with me, the remainder of Wayne's scenes are only with men, no women. And, of course, his heroic character dies of cancer at the end of the movie. John Wayne himself died of cancer just three years later, making for a life-imitates-art ending.

So, apparently, I am very well-known in Japan—not for my work, but for whom I worked *with*!

It couldn't have been a greater pleasure!

12

DING DONG

In all my excitement over being back to work, I'd paid very little attention to the fact that my grandmother was dying. She had diagnosed herself with breast cancer but was unwilling to see a real doctor about it. Some might think me cruel, but I used this as an opportunity to plan my escape.

There was one thing I needed in order to move out. Money. I had *some*. I needed more. She'd told me she kept my childhood money in a private trust account. I needed to figure out a way to close out that account. So I stole her passbook. Back in the day, before certain modern conveniences were invented, bank account holders were given a "passbook" to their account. Small, maybe 3x4", easily carried in one's purse, one would hand this passbook to the bank teller for her (and yes, back then, they were all women) to update each transaction. One would be helpless to make a deposit or withdrawal without it. So, passbook in hand, I drove the few blocks to the bank and took a deep breath.

"Good morning," I said timidly as I stepped to a kind-looking teller. "My name is Melody Thomas and I would like to close a private trust held in my name."

I was taking a gamble. In truth, I did not know if my grandmother had been honest. Did I even have a private trust? She'd given me some of my money. Had she spent the rest?

The bank teller left the window and searched through a few file cabinets before returning. "Yes." She nodded. "There is a private trust here in your name. However, in order to withdraw money or close out the account, the one who opened it must give their consent."

There was money! There *was* a trust. I breathed a sigh of relief. I then put on my best performance to date, explaining tearfully how my dear, sick, old grandmother was unable to get out of bed.

Now something like this could never happen today, but for whatever reason—maybe I just looked trustworthy?—this teller decided to draw up the papers to close out the account. All I needed to do was to get my grandmother to sign the paperwork. Remotely. I could bring back the signed papers and the money would be mine.

That is exactly what happened. I went home and went upstairs to my grandmother's room. She was so sick, I remember that she was unable to really write her name. She weakly scribbled something onto the pages I thrust at her. Of course I didn't tell her what I was doing. I made up some lie about a work contract and she trusted what she was signing. Then I went back to the bank and meekly slid the signed forms across the counter. The teller studied the signature and *released* the money to me. All of it. Just at my word. She accepted it. It was an exciting amount of money. There was really no way for me to know if it was *all* of my money, but it didn't matter. It was enough for what I needed.

Back in those days, parents weren't required to save their show-biz kid's money. I had many peers who, when they turned eighteen, discovered that there was no money. I'm talking millions of dollars, just gone. Their parent had spent every single penny. Even today, only a *percentage* of a child's money has to be legally held in trust. So there are, to this day, parents benefiting inappropriately from their child's earnings. I say that to acknowledge that for all my grand-mother didn't do, I thank her for doing *this*. Because this money gave me the security I needed to move away from her.

I'll never forget that first taste of freedom. The feeling was so overwhelming and all-consuming. The apartment I moved into was nothing fancy—a tiny, furnished single in Van Nuys. But you couldn't have convinced me it was anything short of paradise. When I made the final trip into *my new* home with the few belongings I needed (mostly clothes), and closed the door behind me, I literally started jumping up and down with joy. No friends were with me. It was just me. In my new tiny home, screaming my head off. But the realiza-tion was mind-blowing. I would no longer be a victim to *her*. No lon-ger would my happiness be determined by her ever-changing mood swings, melt-downs, tantrums, and violence. I had escaped a living hell. At last. I'm not sure I've ever known such a feeling of joy since. In fact, I know I haven't. I was on such a high. Years later I would come down to Earth and realize the emotional impact those years of abuse had on my mental health, but we'll get more into that later. For now it's enough to know that I was extraordinarily happy. It truly *was* the first day of the rest of my life.

Several months later I had to return to the house to pick up some items forgotten in my initial haste. I stepped into my childhood home. Nothing had changed. Why would it have? I climbed up the olive green carpeted stairs and moved slowly down the hall toward her bedroom. I didn't really *want* to see her. Didn't want to be there, either. I suppose I was doing the "right" thing. Even though for so many years she had denied me "right" or even normal.

I pushed open the door and stepped into her small, stuffy bed-room. Dusty boxes, stacks of papers, magazines, broken appliances, combs and brushes, trash, and piles of dirty clothes covered every square inch. The downstairs portion of the house was filthy, but my grandmother's bedroom was worse. It was an indoor junkyard right on the outskirts of Larchmont Village.

I could see my grandmother lying on her twin-sized bed, with her breasts exposed. This wasn't shocking. I was used to seeing her breasts on display. Within the house, her outfit of choice was a muddy brown girdle that, believe it or not, had once been white. What *was* shocking this day was that her breasts were covered in something black, like tar. I knew that she'd been seeing some kind of Christian Science healer in her attempt to avoid seeing an actual doctor. I didn't really know then what a Christian Science healer was. I only knew that in their sessions, the "healer" would touch her and "pray" away her breast cancer. Then, according to my grandmother, the cancer disappeared . . . or something. At that particular moment, I concluded that the black muck covering her chest must have been some sort of spiritual Windex, gifted from the "healer," intended to clean away the disease for good.

I scooted around the stacks of clutter to stand at her bedside. Her Edith Bunker-style brown wig had been removed, revealing to me, for the first time, sparse strands of white-gray hair. I immediately started babbling away about a movie-of-the-week I had just been cast in, the studio, and the shoot dates. She only grunted in response, so I looked down at her in exasperation as if to say, *can't you show some enthusiasm?* But my brow instantly furrowed. There were baby worms moving in and around the muck on her chest. Another gift from the Christian Scientist? Another one of her healing "remedies"?

Worms?

I stumbled back, straight into her dresser, knocking some of her trash onto the floor.

"There . . . are baby *worms* on you." I exclaimed.

"They're not worms!" she hissed, glaring at me with a hate-tinged side eye. "They're magnets."

My grandmother wasn't the sharpest tool in the shed. Her mispronunciations were a commonality, but this particular mispronunciation did guide me to clearly surmise that what I was gazing upon were maggots. *Maggots!* There were living, breathing maggots burrowing through her flesh. This wasn't some sort of spiritual Windex, or a black slime gift from the nutty scientist. This was rotting *skin*. I was totally aghast. Who would allow this to happen to their body?

I covered my nose. The stench was more than I could stomach. I had never smelled a decomposing human body before, but I imagined that it would smell something like the odor that was emanating from my grandmother...like a carcass on a scorching summer sidewalk. It was all encompassing, as if scent had found form and was able to attack you with invisible hands and penetrate like a knife to the gut.

Oh, and there were flies—actual flies hovering above her body. Like vultures in the desert, circling a wounded animal, waiting for the cold hand of death to descend, so that they could, at last, devour their prey.

Perhaps I touched her on a patch of living skin and assured her that things would be okay. Though if I did, I certainly knew that things would *not* be okay. She was dying. Whether or not *she* knew it, I knew it.

I didn't feel sad that day as I drove away in my Chevy Nova, nor was I surprised when I did finally get the call. Don't imagine some sort of dramatic scene where I burst into tears, realizing how much I loved her and would miss her. It didn't happen. There was *no* love lost.

When we got to the chapel on the day of her funeral, it was an open casket. She had no friends so it was only our small family, in a gorgeous, giant chapel, with empty pews. Uncle Sven was there, as was my grandfather, who was in the final stages of Alzheimer's at this point and seemed confused as to what was even occurring. My biological mother made a rare appearance as well. And, of course, the dearly departed herself, looking better than I'd ever seen her look when she was alive.

Most of the service was a blur, though I can recall the moment when my grandfather finally made the connection that it was his wife lying in the casket. You could almost see his mind unlock. Since I never saw any love between the two, I thought he'd be just as unfeeling as I was to see an end to life under her rule, so I found it rather telling when he began to weep. Perhaps he'd loved her after all.

As for me? This was the day I had been anticipating and longing for, for well over a decade. My sentence with her had been served. I was granted freedom. Only I felt nothing. No excitement. No joy. If anyone had dared asked me to speak, I probably would have stood, shrugged, and said something similar to: *Um . . . ding dong the witch is finally dead, I guess.* And then quickly sat back down.

Thank goodness they didn't ask.

13

THE YOUNG
AND THE SHIRTLESS

I must tell you. John Landis used to hate me. Maybe he still does!
On Friday, September 15, 1978, I was called in to audition for
Animal House. For the initial meetings, I talked to Bob Edmondson,
who was the senior casting executive for Universal. We got on fine—
Bob was great. A real charmer. I was thrilled and had great feelings
about the movie itself. It seemed like a fun, happy college film. Of
course, no one knew how big of a deal *Animal House* would be, or the
sort of reputation it would gain over the years. At the time I was in-
terviewing, I hadn't even read the script.

When all the auditions were said and done, I was offered the role
of Mayor's Daughter and finally given access to the full script. I read
and read, slowly turning the pages in my bed.

Topless?!

I reached out to my agent.

"Oh, Diane?"

"Yes, honey. Are you happy about the offer?!"

"*Well . . .*" I started.

I explained my trepidation. Appearing topless in a movie? No,
thank you. To this day I've never appeared topless on screen. And
I've played a stripper!

"If it can't be adjusted, Diane," I said seriously, deciding for the first time to stand my ground, "then I'm afraid I'll have to pass."

I was actually in Diane's office when she made the call, explaining to John Landis the particulars of why I did not want to do a topless scene. I was so nervous sitting there, waiting to hear his response. When you're an actress trying to find your footing, turning down parts is no small thing. And I could tell by Diane's expression that he was not taking too kindly to the news.

"He's spitting bullets!" she whispered, covering the receiver so he wouldn't hear our conversation. "He's really set on *you* playing the part."

I was flattered, sure, but unwilling to budge. John begged my agent to talk some sense into me. For days he ranted and raved to my agent via phone calls before finally giving up. He did however, have some parting words for me.

"He says he never wants to see you in his casting office again. And you'll never be cast in any of his films," Diane explained. "End quote."

Well, I thought. *Temper, temper, John Landis!* Of course, *Animal House* turned out to be a smashing success. But *please* don't think I shed even a single tear over my breasts missing their film debut. Instead, I was relieved and thrilled to move on.

Later in life I've told a few friends about my incident with Landis. They've typically responded with shock, saying something like, "You turned down a film with John Landis? How did you have the courage to do such a thing?"

First of all, I had no idea who John Landis was at the time. To me, he was just a director. A director who I didn't want shooting live footage of my breasts. Was he even famous then? I didn't know. But it wouldn't have mattered if he were the most famous director in the galaxy. I was actually amused by how upset he was. My agent shared each and every enraged word he spoke to her about me. I just remember thinking, *Surely there have to be tons of young, blonde actresses who'd be delighted to have this role. Why me?* He was so set on *me*. Was it his pride? Had he never been turned down before? I had no idea. I only knew he was *tremendously* upset. I thought it rather silly.

To this day I've never gone shirtless for any project. When it comes to baring your body, if it's not something you're comfortable doing, you're just not comfortable doing it. Though I must admit, I was once approached to do a cover and photospread for *Playboy*. When I was forty-seven! I was so flattered and, well, amused, that I took the meeting at their very famous offices on Sunset Boulevard. I had absolutely no intention of getting naked for *Playboy*, but it was a fun meeting. Later we turned down the offer very graciously *and* respectfully.

But I will say one last thing about John Landis: he made good on his word. I was never invited to audition or work for him again.

That's Hollywood.

14

THE FURY

It was June 1977, and I had an interview at 20th Century Fox with Brian DePalma, the director responsible for *Mission Impossible*, *Carlito's Way*, *The Untouchables*, *Scarface*, and many more. Of course, back in the late seventies, Brian was mostly known for directing *Carrie*, the Steven King book-to-film adaptation that changed the world of horror films forever. It featured Sissy Spacek and a giant bucket of pigs' blood.

Pigs' blood aside, my very first interview was with Brian himself and Amy Irving, the star of the movie. Brian was very much a "throw the script down and let's improv" kind of director, which suited me fine. Plus Brian seemed to take a liking to me right away, which also suited me fine. When he asked me to stay to read with some of the girls auditioning for other roles, I happily agreed.

I should be honest. I hadn't seen the movie *Carrie*, so I didn't know who Amy Irving even was. Not that it would have made much of a difference anyway. I had the sort of personality where it didn't matter who you were, I was going to be unfiltered and friendly regardless.

"So do you have a boyfriend?" I remember asking Amy during one of our audition breaks.

"I do," she said.

"Oh really? What does he do?"

"Mmm . . . He's a director," she said.

"Oh, really? What's he directed?" I asked nonchalantly, as if gabbing with a friend from school.

I could feel her unwillingness to answer my nosy question. She
murmured quietly, " . . . *Jaws*."

Jaws? I certainly knew who Steven Spielberg was. *This girl must be
somebody special,* I remember thinking. *She's dating one of the most
famous directors in the world!* She would, of course, go on to marry
Steven Spielberg, but that, I'm afraid, is not my story to tell.

I ended up being cast in *The Fury* as LaRue, best friend to Amy's
Gillian Bellaver. Amy and I became fast friends during our time
filming in Chicago. Or maybe she just couldn't fling me off! I stuck
to her like glue, mesmerized by all that she was. Amy was sophisticated, savvy, world-traveled. Her father was a famous theater director and producer and her mother a well-known actress. Her best
friend was *Carrie Fisher*. She traveled in circles not only with Steven
Spielberg, but also with Harrison Ford, George Lucas . . . I mean,
Laurence Olivier was one of her family friends. To say she was out of
my league would be a *gross* understatement.

In addition to forming a bond with Amy, the entire cast and crew
became quite close. We'd play poker in the evenings up in Executive
Producer Frank Yablans's penthouse suite where "everybody" was
doing *everything*. I hate to dismiss the drug scene with a casual *oh,
but it was just the times.* But . . . it was the times! Still, I had never
experienced this scene face to face in my youth and here it was, presented to me for the first time. Not to sound like a goody two shoes,
because I'm no angel, but I never did join in on *that* particular part
of our cast bonding. No judgment for those who chose to go under
the influence of drugs, though. I simply never trusted what drugs
would do to me.

For more innocent fun, we could always count on John Cassavetes, who seemed to know Chicago like the back of his hand. He was always surprising us with impromptu dinners at amazing Italian restaurants. But there's one outing he treated us to that's hard even for me to believe all these years later, and I was there!

The King Tut exhibit was at Chicago's Field Museum at that time. Between our shooting schedule and the long lines at the museum, there was no way that any of us would be able to take a quick peek at King Tut. But it was a huge tour and the whole city was talking about it, and we desperately wanted to go.

One night—I believe it was a Saturday—Cassavetes treated us to yet another meal at an award-winning Italian restaurant. But our dinner was much later than usual, and we didn't leave the restaurant until around 11:30 p.m. After climbing into our waiting studio vans, our drivers followed strict instructions on where to take us next. We were not going back to the Continental Plaza Hotel yet.

To this day I don't know how he did it, but Cassavetes had made arrangements with who knows how many museum contacts and employees. At midnight, our vans pulled up to a back entrance at the Field Museum; we got out, having been prepped in the vans to keep our voices down and do *exactly* as we were told. Abracadabra, and poof! We were taken into a private back hallway of the museum. Hocus pocus, and poof! We were ushered into its great public rooms by silent security guards. The next step was a bit trickier, as we had to bend down and jump over invisible alarm beams. I know! Seems preposterous, entirely made up, like something out of a spy movie—but I was there. We did indeed see the King Tut exhibit that night, and afterwards were whisked into our waiting vans as secretly as we had arrived, then on to our hotel. Another unbelievable evening courtesy of John Cassavetes! It was certainly one of my most memorable filming experiences.

The film was coming to an end and we all worked hard to finish the location scenes in Chicago, including a sequence shot at a real high school where actual students were cast as extras. One of those extras was a young girl named Daryl Hannah. She wasn't known at the time, but years later I thought, *my goodness! That's the girl who played one of the extras at the girl's school.* Watch the film very closely and I bet you can spot her!

As is often the case, my friendship with Amy came to an end as soon as the shoot did. But the thrill of working with Brian DePalma became one of the highlights of my career. Boy, what a talented director. He is such a master collaborator that he manages to not only make all cast and crew comfortable, but compels them to bring their absolute best to the table, in order to assist him in his ultimate vision. Not an easy feat to pull off. I was disappointed that *The Fury* didn't do very well with the critics or the box office. But I wouldn't have given up this wonderful experience for all the gold in the King Tut exhibit!

PART II

★

NIKKI REED

15

THE YOUNG
AND THE REPLACED

I 'm not the original Nikki.

Now I can't get into the particulars of *why* the show was looking for a replacement back in 1979, but rumor had it the original
Nikki had some . . . issues on set. I'm putting it mildly. Apparently
quite a few complaints were coming in to the executive producer at
the time. Cast members wanted her gone. And so, the search for
someone new began.

Spoiler alert. I got the job. But the devil is in the details!

I'll admit that I'd never seen the show before I got the initial call.
I did the prep work I always do, studying the scenes the night before
as best I could. My audition was well-received by casting director
Trudy Soss, and I was summoned to a callback the following day.
There, I met with the Executive Producer, John Conboy. After running the lines a few times, he leaned forward right there in his office
and asked, "Melody, would you be interested in becoming a member of the company of *The Young and the Restless*?"

In that moment I felt transported. Back to getting my hair braided
by Kirk Douglas at eighteen years old. Was I being offered this role?

"Sure!" I replied simply.

Turns out he couldn't offer me the role. At least not at this stage. A few additional executives needed to chime in first, but it did seem as if John Conboy had cast his vote for me. Still, I was summoned to a screen test where *everyone* would get an opportunity to have their say.

Screen tests are a beast of a situation for actors. On one hand, you are asked to sign contracts before you even shoot the test as if you've gotten the job. You can almost taste victory. You know how much money you will be making; you know what your billing will be; you essentially know the particulars of a life you haven't quite yet earned. Talk about dangling the carrot in front of someone. Actors summoned to screen tests must face a tribunal of judges, if you will. And only *one* can walk away victorious.

Which brings me to the other actress testing for the role, Stephanie Burchfield. I never saw her that day, but I'd often seen her around town at auditions (we were a similar type) and we'd become friends. She was just as lovely and talented as can be. This is what people don't understand about the competitive nature of our business. Sure, only one person can walk away with the role. But that doesn't mean the people who walk away with a shredded contract aren't adequate or should be considered less than. We have a respect for one another. We come to learn and understand final decisions often come down to particulars that are out of our control. Height. Hair color (hello . . . bleached bottle blonde at eight years old). In the end it's rarely a matter of being better than someone. More so, it's about serving the needs of the character and the network's and creator's vision.

The morning of my screen test, after a blocking and rehearsal session with director Richard Dunlap in the historic CBS TV City rehearsal halls, I was taken downstairs to the soundstage, Studio 41. I wasn't nervous. I really never was nervous for any auditions or screen tests. I just did the best I could and immediately tried to forget about it. It doesn't serve you or the people around you to fret and obsess about an outcome that you have no control over.

One of my test scenes was with Nikki's sister Casey, played by Roberta Leighton. I must say, there are some people who, the minute you meet them, you know you'll be great friends. You sort of sense a lifetime bond. That's how I felt the moment I met Roberta. Our scenes together were *effortless*.

I also had scenes with Beau Kayser, who played Brock. Nikki was an obnoxious teen from the wrong side of the tracks with quite the attitude—a bit of a departure for me as I had always played the sweet, innocent girl next door until that day. Beau couldn't have been sweeter, making me feel comfortable with this "new" soap medium. Well, it was new for me!

There was no point in speculating about my performance. That only makes the waiting worse. So instead I tried to not think about it at all, which I'll admit was easy. Want to know why? I was up for another show—an NBC pilot for a sitcom called *Highcliffe Manor*. I'll admit that I wanted the sitcom. It was a comedy and I was anxious to channel my inner Lucille Ball.

I didn't hear about the results of the *Y and R* screen test for a day or two. Remember, this was before the internet and emailing video files in seconds. Bill Bell and his co-creator wife, Lee, lived in *Chicago*, so the tapes—yes, *tapes*—had to be put on a plane and sent to O'Hare Airport. The Bells would then view them and phone John Conboy at CBS with their decision.

In the meantime, the sitcom *was* offered to me, so I put *The Young and the Restless* out of my mind. Until I received a call from my agent, that is.

"Well, you got *The Young and Restless*," she said. "Your first day is Monday and they need you to sign a three-year contract. They said the other actress was prettier but that you were the better actress."

Whoa . . . why did Diane always have to be so honest?

"But what about the pilot?" I asked.

She explained that, legally, if an actor gets two contract jobs simultaneously, they can only do one. *I* had to choose. And I had only a few hours to make a choice. I was about to turn down a contract role. But which one? Diane talked me into taking the job with CBS.

In the blur of this bounty of riches I almost forgot about what would happen to my recurring role on *The Waltons*. I had been playing the role of Darlene Jarvis, girlfriend and future wife of Ben Walton (played by Eric Scott). I loved the cast and crew and would have stayed there forever, but it wasn't a contract role, so if I took *Y and R* it would mean the end of my time at *The Waltons*.

Though I was still torn about the sitcom, there was no guarantee that it would ever advance past the pilot stage. With Diane's guidance I made a choice based on *wisdom*.

Stability.

Financial freedom.

Community.

Normalcy.

Poor Diane had to work pretty hard on me, but of course I chose to do *Y and R.*

It was a whirlwind from there. The call from Wardrobe came almost immediately. Hair and makeup needed to see me, too. I had to drive to TV City to be fitted for the clothes I'd be wearing in just a few days. Scripts were already available for the following week. There were introductions to cast, crew, and executives. It was everything all at once. I barely had time to process what was happening.

I was the newest cast member of the successful daytime drama, *The Young and the Restless*.

I was the new Nikki . . . Now what?!

16

THE LONE STRIPPER
OF DAYTIME TELEVISION

Nikki's done *a lot* in Genoa City. Let's recount some of the more harrowing tales:

She's been widowed.
Killed her father (as he was trying to rape her).
Drunk herself into a stupor. Many times.
Had affairs. Many times.
Gone to rehab. A few times.
She's been shot.
Left her fiancé at the altar.
Killed her best friend.
Married her doctor.
Divorced said doctor.
Been kidnapped. Many times.
Been shot (again).
Suffered from a debilitating disease. A few times.

And *much, much more.* I don't have enough pages to list it all! But of all the storylines that have taken Nikki into new territory, I have to admit that the stripping was one of my least favorite, albeit the one most fans mention first!

Here's how it happened: After only about a year of playing Nikki, I was summoned to our Executive Producer John Conboy's office. This sort of thing never happened on our production unless one was being let go. *Oh, no,* I thought, *I'm being fired.*

After being ushered into his office, I sat down opposite him, resigned to why I was there. John started talking, and I wasn't really listening; just waiting for the lowering of the boom. I soon realized that it didn't really sound like I was being fired . . . by the time I actually tuned in to his words, he was saying, "So how would you feel about Nikki being a mud wrestler?"

What? Mud wrestler? I *wasn't* being fired? I was so relieved I instantly agreed to it.

I left his office with a spring in my step, planning to visit the popular mud wrestling clubs on Sunset Boulevard for research! I only had time to observe a couple of them when, the next week, John called me to his office again. It turned out that as soon as CBS learned of the mud wrestling plan, they nixed it. Bill Bell had an immediate backup plan: How did I feel about Nikki becoming a stripper? Not considering the mechanics of such a venture, I immediately told John, "No problem!"

As soon as I agreed, scripts were written and preparations were made. There is no time to waste in the making of daytime television. At that time, we shot only one week before airing. *Y and R* had also recently expanded to an hour-long format.

Before I knew it, a copy of the song that had been selected for the first strip, Donna Summer's "Love To Love You Baby," was given to me on a cassette. I would use it to learn the routine, rehearsing it endlessly in the rehearsal hall and some more at home. Choreographers were hired to make me look as proficient at stripping as I could. Due to my training going back to the Meglin Kiddies, I was familiar with learning a dance routine through a series of "eights." For each count of eight of the music, you learn a corresponding move. And it's not just your feet you have to think about!

One: Strut left.
Two: Pop right hip.
Three: Step forward left.
Four: Step forward right.
Five: Take right earring off.
Six: Left shoulder roll with boa.
Seven: Pull dress open from right Velcro band.
Eight: Toss right glove to audience facing Camera Left.

And so forth and so on . . . Your mind is swimming with counting the eights and successfully executing the corresponding moves, facing the correct cameras, saying dialogue, all the while making everything seem natural, effortless, and fluid.

Now before I continue, I must say, to all the strippers of the world—what you do isn't easy. It's an art most women aren't capable of executing elegantly. I turned out to fit into the category of most women. When my choreographer, Carol Conners, would dance the routine for me, it was beautiful. When I would run through it, it felt and looked awkward. I just didn't have the natural fluidity.

But the storyline was so salacious for that time, it didn't really matter that I wasn't Sally Rand (famous fan dancer and stripper)! Fans seemed to not notice my shortcomings and just loved to carry on about the fact that Nikki was STRIPPING! In a dive club! *Oh, no, Nikki, please snap out of it and get yourself on the right path!*

The fans have always supported Nikki, felt for her, rooted for her, no matter what fix she gets herself into. And, because of the censors' constraints at the time, no one seemed to notice or care that Nikki always wore pantyhose for those strip routines.

But, boy, were they popular! I don't think I realized at the time just how popular they were. Each week when the scripts arrived I'd turn the pages just to get an idea of what Nikki would be up to next, and there it would be: Nikki strips.

Over and *over* again, every week, I was up on that stage on the Bayou set ripping off clothes set by Wardrobe with secret tearaways and Velcro. I did struggle with occasional moments of feeling like a fraud. I never felt I had the inherent sexiness that Nikki needed to have. I became convinced I wasn't pulling it off (sorry, pun intended). But perhaps I was wrong. Because Bill Bell *kept* writing it.

Here's a fun fact I never knew until my fortieth anniversary party: Brad Bell (Bill Bell's son) gave a speech spilling the deets. He was a teenager during the stripper era (as I fondly refer to it), and he didn't much care for daytime soaps. But his family used to get the day's tapes from the airport every evening and sit with their dinner in the living room, watching the show as they ate. That way, Bill could have time to call and make any changes before the episodes were set to air. Brad was a teenaged boy at this time and oh boy, did his interests shift when Nikki's stripper episodes premiered in his living room. In fact—he's now the Executive Producer/Head Writer of *The Bold and the Beautiful*! Family time watching *The Young and the Restless* as a teenager pushed him to follow in his parents' footsteps. I like to think I played some role in that. Literally. I mean, after all, it was Nikki's striptease that first got him to pay attention.

I digress.

No matter what the reason, the stripping continued. It actually became the vehicle through which Nikki met Victor Newman. This was probably part of Bill's plan from the very beginning, though neither Eric nor I had any idea of that. We were both bewildered as to why the villainous-but-wealthy Victor Newman would be interested in Nikki when he could have had practically any other woman on the planet! Nikki was raw, unsophisticated, and uneducated, lacking in all social graces. But, my, did that set up that fun *Pygmalion* story perfectly! As always, Bill knew *exactly* what he was doing.

I'm reminded of one of the funnier takes that never made it to the airwaves: Years after the initial strips, Jack takes Nikki to the Colonnade Room for an elegant evening. Nikki, more than a bit tipsy, ends up doing an impromptu striptease right there on the dance floor. The Colonnade Room was pure sophistication; the men were in tuxedos, and Nikki was wearing a beautiful floor-length gown. But oh, *Nikki.* If memory serves me correctly, she spots Victor in the dining room and resolves to show him what he has given up. Sloppily drunk, she decides ripping off her clothes is the best way to get Victor's attention.

At least that's what the script said . . . Here's what actually happened: I'm doing my drunken routine and making a scene. Literally. Finally, I get to the part where I'm supposed to tear off my dress and kick it to a ringside table. I do. But when I kick it, it suddenly grows wings and flies straight up. Right to the crystal chandelier hanging directly above me! So there it is hanging, like a stalactite. Not knowing if production saw this gaffe, I just keep doing my dance in my skimpy lingerie with my dress hanging above my head!

In 1984, Nikki's stripping improved. I mean . . . *greatly* improved. Mostly because I wasn't the Nikki who was stripping; I'd been replaced. It's not as juicy as it sounds. Here's what happened.

I had been dealing with increasing fatigue for weeks with no real clue as to what was wrong with me. There was finally a day, shooting in the Colonnade Room, where my only job was to sit in a full-length gown and look pretty. I didn't even have any dialogue. But that particular day I was growing weaker and weaker as the work hours dragged on. Even sitting under the lights was too strenuous for me. Overcome with exhaustion, I began to cry.

The crew rushed me off the set to my dressing room where I immediately collapsed. I was taken to a doctor. Blood tests showed I was suffering from three different immune-destroying viruses: Epstein-Barr, mononucleosis, and something called cytomegalovirus, CMV for short. The only cure for all three? Bed rest. So that's what I had to do. But the show had to go on. And so a temporary Nikki was hired.

During my time off, I tuned in to *Y and R* every day from bed. Temporary Nikki was a *fabulous* stripper! It was a surreal experience watching her work. She was a real natural on the Bayou stage. Rather than feel intimidated, I started taking mental notes. When I returned to work I was more determined than ever to tackle stripper Nikki and make my interpretation just as good. But alas. I just didn't . . . have it.

I have looked back at it. Mostly because people send me clips. Thanks, Twitter and Instagram. A ton of clips. The clips never end. I maintain that I was not very good, but I also maintain the stripping propelled Nikki's story to where it needed to go. I acknowledge Bill's genius. I wouldn't change it. Not for the world. But eventually (thank the soap opera gods), Nikki *did* stop stripping—though the writers would occasionally find a way to work it into a scene. But one day I ended the stripper era for good. I was forty-eight, and our head writer at the time was Jack Smith. I was in hair and makeup one day when he called.

"Hi, Jack, what's up? What can I do for you?"

"You know, Mel, I was thinking. Wouldn't it be great to have you strip again?"

I think I laughed. And everyone in the room could hear my side of the conversation when I followed up with, "Jack. I am forty-eight years old. I'm not stripping!"

There was a quite a bit of, "Oh, but you look so good!" and blah blah *blah*. Producers and writers will try to talk you into anything! That day I stood my ground. And Nikki the stripper died.

May she rest in peace.

Still, the fans will always remember the stripping. They *loved* it. Especially the male ones. I'm pretty confident there's never been another stripper on daytime television—probably because of my great inability to do it!

While I can't play a stripper, fans of the show are convinced that there is one dramatic form in which I particularly excel: playing a drunk Nikki. It's true I resisted stripper Nikki, but I simply *adore* her drunk counterpart.

Is it because I'm a terrible drunk myself? I've been known to enjoy a drink from time to time, sure, but I can hardly scratch the surface of Nikki's dramatic plunge into the abyss. I think I enjoy playing Drunk Nikki so much because for me, it's a chance to add a bit of comedy to *Y and R*.

As far as onscreen comedy, I have done a few: *My Name is Earl* and *The Crazy Ones*, with Robin Williams, right before he passed. I think it's very hard for this town to see me as funny because of the soap pigeonhole I'm in. But I *can* be funny! I remember a casting reading for a feature film that the iconic comedy genius, Carl Reiner, was doing years ago. He kept laughing hard at my performance there in his office. I didn't get the part but I've always said that I want my tombstone to read, *Carl Reiner Thought She Was Funny*. I *did* get to do *The Vagina Monologues* on stage. What a thrill that was. To me there is nothing more satisfying. Getting to make the audience laugh *and* cry. It was a wonderful experience.

So I suppose Drunk Nikki is my way to connect to an element of comedy. Being sloppy drunk is so embarrassing and so abysmal, you can't help but laugh. The slurring of the words, so loose you can't even *remember* your lines let alone walk in a straight one, the over-articulation so people don't *think* you're drunk when clearly, you're very drunk.

Alcoholism isn't something I've struggled with, but most people have at some point in their lives been drunk and I'm certainly one of them. I will admit that our entire cast and crew would venture across the street to a bar during dinner breaks. Many years ago, before The Grove was built next door, we'd cross Fairfax Avenue to a place called Kelbo's. Kelbo's is no more, but oh, if its walls could talk. They would've said: *Pssst! The entire cast and crew of Y and R gets drunk here! And then they go back to work! Still drunk!*

The crew, directors, the cameramen. It was almost *everyone*. Looking back, I think, *How on earth did we manage to finish the show that day?* But we did. We sobered up enough to finish that day's episode. So perhaps there were *some* moments (maybe one or two) in the eighties, when Tipsy Nikki was being guided by Tipsy Mel!

Kelbo's plays a role in some of my fondest moments from those years. It's where I first started getting to know my future husband Edward—but we'll get to that later. And those years were heavy in establishing the Victor and Nikki storyline. One of the first daytime TV power couples—Niktor.

When scripts started coming my way pairing Nikki Reed and Victor *Newman* . . . I simply couldn't wrap my mind around it. Why us? We were the least likely pair. For starters Nikki was, well, a stripper, and I think Victor, at the time, may have been keeping his wife's lover in the basement and feeding him rats. Yes, I think that might be right. Anyway, I remember thinking . . .

Victor and Nikki? What on Earth is wrong with Bill Bell?

But Bill could be prescient with these things. He was quite the genius when it came to *Y and R* storylines and pairings. We were an unlikely duo but it did make for good TV. Once I entered Victor's life, the viewers started to see a very different side of him—sweet, caring, falling in love with Nikki.

The development of Nikki and Victor did happen very slowly. I don't think any of us were expecting the storyline to be such a fan favorite or that Bill Bell would continue with the pairing for so *many* years. That's the thing about working on soaps, though. You'd be a fool to try to predict where your storyline is going. It's a very vague area we don't bother putting effort into. We're all on a ride and don't know the final destination. Ever. So if you're an actor that needs to know the destination—better stick to films. Because in the world of daytime TV, anything is possible.

Any outcome.

Any pairing.

Endless possibilities.

I always assume wherever I end up is where I'm supposed to go. And sure, there have been times I've disagreed or longed for a storyline to end. But the Nikki-and-Victor storyline has not been one of them. I like to think of Victor as Henry Higgins and Nikki as Genoa City's Eliza Doolittle. Victor arranged for French lessons, piano lessons, etiquette lessons, horseback lessons, and everything in between to transform her into a "lady."

And Nikki needed all the help she could get!

17

AND THE MOTHER IS . . .

I met Carlos Yeaggy on the set of *The Young and the Restless.* He was my makeup artist, so he tended to see me at my worst: early in the mornings, fumbling into the hair and makeup chair, hair pointing out in all directions, cranky, half-awake.

Carlos worked with me during an era I like to refer to as the *Y and R* glory days, when the makeup artists were truly *artists* practicing their art form. Now it's much more *hurry up and get it done and we'll fix it in post,* so makeup artists don't always get their well-earned opportunities to shine. But back then, it took *time* for Carlos to help transform me into Nikki (believe me, it was no easy feat). So over the time we worked so closely together, we became . . . close.

I don't remember us ever going on dates in the beginning, like to the movies or anything. We mostly started out as great friends. We'd talk for hours. I found him to be quite handsome. Connecting felt completely natural. I believe the first outing I'd dare call a date started off with Carlos stepping to me and asking, "Mel, would you like to go on a picnic with me?"

Picnic? I remember thinking. *What does picnic mean? More than friends? Are we more than friends?*

After that first picnic I suppose I had to admit to myself that we were dating. And after the gloom and doom of two prior failed marriages (I'll get to those later), it was natural, easy, refreshing, and fun. With Carlos, I was happy.

Oh, but I should mention—we kept it a secret. No one on the show knew that we were dating. It's not that our relationship would've been discouraged, but we felt protective of it and didn't want to risk set gossip and everyone being involved in our personal lives.

Instead, I came up with a codename: Richard. I was very young and excited and in *love*—I couldn't resist talking about him to my friends! Most of whom were on the set with me.

"How's Richard?" cast and crew would ask me in the mornings as I was chatting with "Richard" himself!

"Oh, he's wonderful," I'd reply with a sly grin.

Cast and crew did begin to speculate, of course. *Who is Richard? Richard who?!* At the time, *Three's Company* was shooting across the hall from us. I didn't realize it then, but the general consensus was that *my* Richard had to be Richard Kline, who played upstairs neighbor Larry on the show. The funniest thing about this? To this day, I've never even met Richard Kline! But the entire cast of *Y and R* was convinced that we were dating.

Carlos and I continued to grow closer. Our relationship took a giant leap when we decided to move in together. It was at this point that I knew it might be time to let the cat out of the bag. To a few. We invited our dear friend, Patti Denney (another *Y and R* makeup artist), to our house in Sherman Oaks. Patti, another forty-years-plus member of the company, works on the show to this day. She has done my makeup for years and still does. Patti was thrilled to visit on this particular day because I had informed her that Richard would be there and I wanted her to be the first one to meet him.

When Patti rang the doorbell, Carlos ran into the back bedroom. Patti and I hung out in the living room for a little while, casually chatting. Finally she could resist no more. "So, how's Richard?" she asked.

"Well," I said, "He's actually already here. Do you want to say hi to him?"

Did she ever. Finally, she was going to get to meet the mysterious Richard. She followed me down the hall, and when I pushed opened the door, Carlos was sitting on the bed. She couldn't believe it!

Though "Richard" was Carlos and not Richard Kline from *Three's Company*, Patti was thrilled to bits. The makeup team is very close. She knew Carlos well and she was absolutely floored that we'd kept this secret as long as we did.

She asked us if we wanted to continue to keep it under wraps. We trusted Patti to do whatever we asked. But now that one person knew, we suddenly wanted everyone to know! Typically, on any set in Hollywood, if you tell one member of the wardrobe, hair, or makeup team something, everyone else will know a half an hour later. I am grateful to have such wonderful, trustworthy, lifelong friends on our crew. We respect each other and, when necessary, will *absolutely* keep a confidence.

I don't remember telling anyone else, but by the next day, every-body on the set already knew!

On January 18, 1982, our houseguest and good friend Dave Zimmer-man, having recently learned how to read tarot cards, said he wanted to do a reading for me. Now, I've always felt very comfortable with the spirit world, true psychics, true mediums, etc. But this proposi-tion was simply viewed as something fun to do that afternoon.

Dave and I got comfortable in the dining room, chatting, while he shuffled and dealt the cards.

I wasn't that knowledgeable of each card's meaning, nor am I now, but after I picked my cards Dave flipped them over and read them together. When he had a conclusion, he stared at me in shock. "Mel," he said. "You're pregnant."

I laughed. What a ridiculous thing to say—especially from quite the novice tarot reader! "I'm not," I insisted.

"You are! And it's a girl!"

I laughed even harder. "I promise you I'm not!"

In the back of my head, I did know that my period was almost a week late. But it couldn't be true—I couldn't be pregnant.

By the week of January 25, I still hadn't gotten my period, and Dave's tarot-reading skills were proving to be more accurate than I had expected. I went to the doctor for the ultimate test. The results were clear: I *was* pregnant.

For this pregnancy, I was absolutely thrilled—though I'd be lying if I didn't admit how big of a shock it was. Carlos and I were using triple birth control: a condom, a diaphragm, and a contraceptive foam (ask your grandmother!). But I suppose fate has a way of superseding anything.

I had to tell the producers, especially when I started gaining weight. It happened so, so quickly. By February, I had started to balloon.

Now, keep in mind, this was 1982. It wasn't common for women to have babies without husbands, nor was it deemed traditionally acceptable. Farrah Fawcett broke that ground, in a way, when she had her son, Redmond, with Ryan O'Neal. But that hadn't happened yet. And even after, it took years for most people to accept that sort of thing.

There was still a very Puritanical way of thinking about "a poor girl who's in trouble." I'd lived through that reality already, with my first pregnancy. I wasn't going to put myself through that sort of thinking again. Not with this baby. My baby. Our baby.

When I first learned I was pregnant, there was an actress on *General Hospital* who had announced that she was single and pregnant. Just like me. Upon releasing the news, she was promptly *fired*.

In truth, the possibility of losing *my* job didn't concern me. Not that I thought I was irreplaceable—I certainly didn't. It's just that everything about this pregnancy felt fated. Stars, angels, spirit guides—I felt like there was something looking after me, guiding me through. I was happy to accept whatever consequences would come of this experience. I wanted this baby, and I was going to have her no matter what.

At the end of February, I told Wes Kenney, our executive producer. We stood on Stage 41, mere steps from my current dressing room. Wes was so lovely and supportive. It was a great start.

He, in turn, informed the other producers. This included Bill and Lee Bell, who were still living in Chicago. I wasn't that worried. I was just hopeful that everyone would take it as well as Wes had. And if not—well, I'd figure it out.

Before I heard back from Bill, however, I got a call in my dressing room, 41B. I answered, certain it would be Bill, but I was surprised when it turned out to be producer Ed Scott.

"Hi, Melody," he said. "I just heard the news about the baby. Congratulations—I think you're going to be a wonderful mother."

I had no idea what to say. Ed and I, back then—well. We weren't close. We were barely even friends. But I had his support. And that meant a lot to me.

Bill called me the next day. He was just as thrilled as everyone else. A few years later, he did confess to me, "You were the *last* actress I wanted to hear this news from!"

Considering that I was playing the resident stripper, I have to say that his shock was quite understandable. But his brilliance as a writer came shining through. I assumed I'd be doing my scenes hidden behind plants and large handbags for the next several months, but Bill decided to do something else: he wrote my pregnancy *into the show*.

I'd never expected that.

Unknowingly, my pregnancy with Alex kick-started one of the most iconic storylines on the show to date: *Who is the father of Nikki's baby*? And the fans, who were already taking a shine to the early and unlikely pairing of Victor and Nikki, ate it up.

The pregnancy, and the question of whose it was, became a huge moment in the show and pop culture in general. If you've seen the 1983 movie *Mr. Mom*, there are a few scenes of Michael Keaton on the phone, and his side of the conversation includes, "What? The vasectomy didn't take?! . . . I knew it was Victor's!" The question of who fathered Nikki's baby became sort of another "Who Killed JR?" moment. It was something that got people talking; something that mattered to the general viewership.

The news of my pregnancy continued to spread, both on the set and off. I was so grateful that people knew, and that I didn't have to sit in the hair and makeup room feeling silently nauseous with morning sickness, unable to speak a word about why I didn't seem like myself.

What a relief it was to have no more secrets. And to have everyone's support.

As fans learned of my condition, baby gifts began arriving at the studio. I did not receive a single negative fan letter. Pregnancy didn't change my busy schedule—I continued having photo shoots and appearances. Motherhood Maternity offered to clothe both Nikki on the show and me in real life for the duration of the pregnancy.

Late in March, I was asked to be a presenter at the Annual Makeup and Hair Awards at the Pasadena Civic Auditorium. It was a black-tie event, and there was no small amount of effort put into finding a dress that would fit me. I was very clearly pregnant.

Carlos accompanied me to the event. It was our first public function together—fitting, considering the nature of the event! While I was waiting in the wings for my cue, I was shocked to discover that the presenter scheduled to follow me was Bette Davis. She was standing right behind me. My ever-present *uber*-publicist, Bob Olive, managed to quickly arrange an introduction.

Now, I'm not generally star struck—actors are people, after all—but at that moment, I certainly was. I was completely and utterly awestruck. My voice disappeared.

I somehow managed, "Very nice to meet you!" Good God, I had no idea what to say to her. Should I mention the years I'd spent admiring her work? My favorite roles? Anything intelligent . . . none of it found a way out of my mouth.

But, to my surprise, she answered with, "Oh, I know who you are, dear. I watch your show every day. You're a lovely actress. You'll go far."

What? If I was speechless before, there was even less of a chance of me being able to put a sentence together after that. *Bette Davis* watched our show!

A photographer appeared at that moment and took our picture. Alas, I've searched for that photo ever since that night, but I've never been able to find it.

That was the first awareness I had that very prestigious, famous people in the world watched our show. As time went on, this fact would become increasingly clearer.

In the beginning of April, my publicist, Bob Olive, came through with yet another tremendous opportunity: the cover of *PEOPLE* magazine. I would be sharing the cover with Tristan Rogers from *General Hospital* and Lisa Brown from *Guiding Light*. The headline had already been determined: ARE SOAPS TOO SEXY? The cover was to be shot by Tony Costa, a very prolific photographer of the time.

I was the first of the trio to arrive at the studio. When I was introduced to Tony, he seemed confused. He was planning on arranging us in sexy poses, such as one would suspect, given the headline. But, as hard as it is to believe, no one had warned Tony that I was five months pregnant! You can only imagine his shock when I walked in.

Without a word, he scrapped the set-up he had planned on. He went upstairs to the second floor of the studio, grabbed some huge bolts of silk fabric, and hurried back downstairs. Tony hastily arranged the shiny satin on the floor into a sort of bed.

He called to his crew for a ladder and hoisted his camera about twelve feet in the air.

There was no way he could shoot my stomach in a sexy pose—this was 1982, after all—so he decided that the three of us would get under makeshift satin "sheets" and smolder up from the floor.

By the time Tristan and Lisa showed up, the switch had been made and they were none the wiser. When the magazine came out on the stands, it looked like the three of us were under satin sheets, luxuriating in bed. You can't tell from looking at it that I'm pregnant at all, let alone showing as much as I was.

On Saturday, September 11, 1982, I was browsing through garage sales in the Valley when I started feeling sharp pains in my stomach. A quick phone call to my doctor prompted him to ask me to meet him at the hospital, right away.

Carlos was in another part of town on the set of the new show he was working on. I drove to the hospital by myself. It was before my due date and I was shocked—everyone had told me that my first would probably be late. So wrong they were!

My first baby. My little girl. I was going to be a mother. I don't think I can really convey just how thrilled I was to be having her, and it was made all the sweeter by everything I had overcome on my own.

She was born literally a few hours after I was admitted into the hospital. The nurse laid her in my arms. She was barely a minute old.

Though most babies don't, she opened her eyes, wide as could be. I was transfixed. I remember looking into those deep, dark eyes and thinking she must be a very old soul. I knew I'd never loved anyone so much. I never knew I *could* love someone so much.

I was taken to a shared room while my private room was being prepared. The drape was pulled between the beds, and having just given birth, I wasn't really aware that there was even another patient in the room.

The nurse came in to clarify some details. She mentioned the baby's last name, Thomas, and I had to correct her.

"Oh, Yeaggy is the last name. I'm not married to the father."

It sounded simple enough to me.

But when the nurse left, almost instantly, the drape between the room's other occupant and me was yanked back.

A young girl looked at me, wide-eyed, and asked, "You're not married to your baby's father?"

"No," I replied as if it was the most natural thing in the world. "I'm not. Are you?"

She was, and her story spilled out. She was only seventeen and had gotten pregnant by a boy who didn't want to be in the picture. Despite this, her parents insisted that they get married. The teen was (understandably) miserable in her marriage. She asked me how on earth I was allowed to have a baby without marrying the father. Why hadn't my parents forced me?

"Because I don't have parents," I explained, and for once, I was grateful for that. I could make my own decisions, and that was that.

It wasn't *entirely* true—my parents were still alive, both of them, but it wasn't like they knew what I was doing, nor did they care.

"I wish I hadn't married him," the young girl confessed. "I don't love him."

I felt awful about her situation, but there was nothing I could have said or done. That's just how things were back then. I still think about that young girl from the hospital room, even years later. I don't know how that little family worked out, but I'm afraid I have a good idea.

Of course, now that my baby was here, there was the matter of her name. Before she was born, Carlos and I had narrowed the girl names down to either Alexandra or Christina. I knew the moment I looked into her eyes that she was an Alexandra, but Carlos wasn't sure. There had to be some sort of negotiation, and time was running out.

The one factor that worked on my side was that Carlos was working long hours on *Romance Theater*, a short-lived nighttime soap helmed by Producer Bill Glenn. So he could only visit us in the evenings, and the daytime nurses were the ones who were pushing me to put a name on the birth certificate.

"Well?" A young nurse stepped into my room. "Can we add a name yet?"

Hmm. I thought. The choice was between slight deceit or caving into Carlos's wish to name the baby Christina. I'm not sure if it was from my soap influence, or my natural propensity to be the Vice President of Sneaky Switches, to quote an *I Love Lucy* phrase, but with Carlos nowhere in sight, I bit the bullet and declared that the baby's name was Alexandra Danielle Yeaggy. We had long agreed that her middle name would be Danielle, so I was safe there.

I don't regret that decision, even though it may have seemed deceitful. I've spoken to Alex about her name many times and she is infinitely happy that she is an Alexandra.

With the name debacle sorted, my time at the hospital was coming to a close. In 1982, women stayed in the hospital a lot longer than they do today—not that I minded. I had literally never changed a diaper before, or even *held* a baby in my entire life, for that matter. Because of this, I'd arranged to have a baby nurse live with us for the first six weeks to show me the ropes.

Carlos drove us home from the hospital: baby Alex in her newly installed car seat, our baby nurse, Mercedes, and me. I was so, so happy. I knew nothing about raising children or taking care of an infant, but I knew I could do a better job than the one who attempted to raise me.

This I was certain of.

18

KNIGHT IN SHINING ARMOR

Carlos and I were successfully co-parenting. But children have a way of expediting the natural course of a relationship. Though Carlos was a tremendously loving and hands-on father, and we were wonderful, dear friends, we soon realized that our true bond was only one of friendship.

Things ended amicably and I set my focus on Alex and my very busy shooting and publicity schedule. I didn't expect—or need—to fall in love. I *especially* didn't expect to fall in love with one of the producers of the show—especially the one producer I didn't too much care for!

Here's the thing about Edward Scott: from the first moment we met, we didn't exactly mesh. There wasn't any sort of on-set controversy. It was more like, I didn't care for him, and he didn't care for me. For whatever reason, whenever he came or went, I was just . . . "Eh. *Ed*."

That all changed. Obviously. He *is* my husband of thirty-five-plus years, after all!

What happened is that Ed started joining us at the cast's occasional excursions to Kelbo's. Off set he was laid back, insightful, and funny, too. Before I knew it, his personality began to shine through. He became less of an "ugh" and more of a "hmm." I was thinking, *Hey. This guy is actually pretty cute. And he has substance.* He wasn't what I normally went for. In fact, he was a complete 180 from Carlos, but there was just something about him. Something I liked. Something that caught me.

As for how he started changing his mind about me, I'm not sure. Even now! I guess that's something for his own autobiography!

Kelbo's meetups with the cast and crew developed into meetups with just Ed and me. I have a note in one of my old datebooks for a Wednesday night near the end of 1983. It says: Dinner with Ed Scott.

Such a simple entry. I'm sure I thought nothing of it. It could very well have been a business meeting. Who would have ever guessed at that time that I was headed to dinner with the man I'd be married to, all these years later? Ed was so easy to fall in love with, though. He was nothing like what you might expect a Hollywood producer to be like. It's interesting how both of us had to put aside our pre-conceived notions about the other. There was this vast wealth of information and charm, kindness, and compassion. Very cinematic, in hindsight.

I was falling in love. *We* were falling in love. That magical feeling was there. The butterflies. The birds sing more sweetly, colors are more beautiful. You know the all-consuming feeling of falling in love. It really was like something out of a fairytale. I didn't realize he was so funny—he certainly wasn't at work!—and so generous, so genuine. Genuine is rare in this business. But I was learning that Edward was not and still is not your typical Hollywood producer. He was a real person, a real human being. And boy could he make me laugh like no other. You know when you first get together and everything is hysterically funny? That's how it was with us. Laughing and laughing, into the morning.

In the beginning of a relationship you just want to be in each other's airspace. You want to be in that glorious bubble that's

encompassing you. Everyone feels that. But those beginning fireworks aren't going to be there forever. I think perhaps that's why
some people jump from relationship to relationship—they love be-
ginnings. They don't understand that after those initial fireworks,
it takes work to keep the magic going. Edward and I seemed up for
the challenge. For the long haul.

He had a daughter, too, and I had Alex, and we all got on well—
though Alex could have gotten along with anyone, since she was a
baby—but my point is, the family blended. Well. By March of 1984,
we were both as committed to one another as we are today.

No one knew about us (there's that secret relationship again!) in
the beginning. But that all changed at Doug Davidson's (Y and R's
Paul Williams) real-life nuptials. It was a gorgeous wedding, in
beautiful Santa Barbara—Doug was marrying Cindy Fisher, who we
all knew well, as she'd played a role in the Y and R cult storyline.
That's actually how they met. Since Edward and I were both individually invited, we decided this would present the perfect opportunity
for us to "come out," if you will. We went together.

I'm sure there was a lot of whispering about us behind the scenes,
but we were blissfully unaware. People don't usually say cruel things
about you to your face. Instead it was a lot of:

"Oh, that's wonderful!

"We're so happy for you!"

"How delightful!"

But later, there were certain members of the cast who grew cold
to me. One, in particular, was Jeanne Cooper. Jeanne and I had been
great friends before I started seeing Edward. In fact, I did call her
"Mother," the only person I bestowed that title to in my life. But
after Edward and I became public, things just weren't the same between Jeanne and me. I know she has said some things that aren't
entirely true about our relationship, and I think it's due to the fact
that I was with Edward. Regarding the *mystifying* claims about me in

her book, all I can say is that we had a complicated relationship, fueled by paranoia. But we still loved each other very deeply. And regardless of what transpired between us, I miss her desperately and will always love her.

I suppose to some, my relationship with Edward looked like a strategic move. But anyone who knows me well will tell you that I'm hardly strategic. I simply fell in love. More than three decades later our bond has only grown stronger.

Edward asked me to marry him over Christmas in 1984. There wasn't any reason to wait. We were already living together as a family, so marriage just made sense. As the years passed he would do things to keep our marriage fresh and exciting. He would plan all of these unbelievable trips, usually keeping most details a surprise for me. One time, we flew on the Concorde to Paris, and stayed in a beautiful suite at the Ritz. One morning, he woke me up and said, "Get dressed, doll. We have a limo waiting."

So I got dressed and went downstairs. We got in the limo and I literally had no idea where we were going. We arrived at the airport, but I hadn't even packed anything! I had assumed we were going out for brunch. But Edward had planned a flight to *Geneva*.

When we arrived, another limo picked us up and drove us to the watch district. In Europe, a lot of shops shut down for lunch for a few hours, so all of the major stores were closed. We walked up and down the lovely Geneva streets, and I saw the most exquisite watch in the window of Cartier. Once the shops reopened, we went into Cartier to inquire about the watch. I don't remember the price that the salesperson quoted; I just knew that it was *too much*! As I rose out of my chair to head for the exit, Edward handed the clerk his credit card to pay for it. I couldn't believe it. I have pictures from this day of me sitting in Cartier with happy tears streaming down my face! We flew back to Paris immediately after buying the watch, just in time for an elegant dinner at Jules Verne at the Eiffel Tower. And to this day I still have that watch that Edward bought for me so many years ago. I'll treasure it always.

Still, even though we were blissfully happy and in love, rumors on the set continued to grow. One of the more ridiculous rumors was that I was writing my own storylines. Anyone who ever met Bill or Lee Bell would've known better—I had no control over Nikki Newman's plot lines. Some cast members also felt that Ed was being preferential to me as far as show visibility or that there was pillow talk going on between us that I shouldn't be privy to—which I wasn't. To this day, Edward keeps information about the shows he's working on to *himself*. I don't ask. He doesn't tell. We have certainly always had much more to talk about at home than work.

I suppose it's natural to resent a coworker if you feel that they are in a better position than you are. I only wish my coworkers, at the time, had been open to the truth. My relationship with Edward has never been about *Y and R*. It's about partnership and family. It's about a genuine bond of love.

19

WE'RE MAKING STORIES

While shooting a movie in Utah back in 1976, I saw the future. The film was called *The Car*. It was about, well, a car. Not just any car, but a possessed, demonic one that was trying to kill people! A Universal Pictures production, it was shot in and around St. George, Utah. A small detail: I almost died there. I'll explain.

The scene in question took place on a dangerous curve of mountain. A precarious part of Zion National Park where a misstep could cause one to plummet over the edge. The jagged rocks hundreds of feet below would have done little to cushion my fall. Imagine it: On this dangerous curve of mountain, I was on a bike, racing at *top* speed. Oh . . . and the possessed, driverless *car* was chasing after me.

At least in theory.

"You're not getting close enough to the edge!" the director, Elliot Silverstein, raged at me after each take.

"Back to one!" Elliot would cry, rolling his eyes in my direction as if I was the bane of his very existence.

I'd be forced to mount the bike once again, palms sweating, heart racing.

The thought did cross my mind that perhaps a stuntwoman might be better equipped to risk her life for this shot. But the director had touched a part of me that, when pushed too far, pushes back. *I was doing this.*

I'll show him, I thought.

On the last take of that sequence, I rode the bike as close to the edge as I ever had. A millimeter more and I would have gone over, no doubt about it.

"Cut!" Elliot cried, aghast, with his hands holding his head, as I rounded the curve and screeched to a stop.

Happy to be alive, I jumped off the bike, handing it off to a crew-member whose jaw was almost to the ground, staring at me with wide-eyed admiration. I dusted myself off and walked over to Elliot with a smug look of satisfaction on my face.

"Close enough?" I asked sweetly.

That was my moment. I almost *killed* myself to say that to him.

In addition to death-defying acts, the tiny town of St. George, Utah, also gave me a tiny glimpse into my future. It would be a few years before I won the role of Nikki on *The Young and the Restless*, but I *had* filmed a couple of episodes of *General Hospital* as Laura's (played by Genie Francis) babysitter. Back then the gig on *General Hospital* was just another job. I knew nothing about soaps at the time and admittedly never even saw the episodes air. But in St. George, Utah, *they'd* seen the episodes. It was as if some big-time celebrity had made it to their town. I witnessed the exuberance and power of daytime drama fans for the first time.

"You were on my story!" they screeched when I arrived at the motel. (There were no hotels in St. George.)

I had never heard it put that way. A *story*. But today I can't agree more. Making daytime dramas is different than traditional filmmaking. We *are* creating stories.

Knowing and understanding (and experiencing first hand) the way fans react to and appreciate soap operas is pretty contrary to the way the film industry views us. Back in the days when soaps first started on television after many successful years of radio, the shows' creators wanted very dramatic character arcs with a high emotional impact. They were catering to their intended audience, primarily housewives. They knew there was a large demographic of women at home raising children, cooking, and cleaning. That's why they're called soaps: the original sponsors were soap companies—Ivory, Palmolive, and Tide, to name a few. These sponsors reflected the viewership: housewives buying soap. Dramatic storylines were meant to appeal to a particular type of woman. Women who were most likely desperate for an alternate and (let's be honest) sometimes ridiculous reality to escape to. Soaps still exaggerate. It heightens the drama of the story. But when you compare that to a fine theater or film actor, who does not overplay, you see a dramatic difference. You should. It's a different kind of acting.

Think about it. If you are a prestigious film producer working on a serious film and just so happen to come across a soap opera clip, you're going to laugh.

There's a demon-possessed woman chained up in the basement.

Someone turns into a jaguar.

Or a zombie.

An entire town is murdered.

Some lunatic steals frozen embryos and inserts them into . . . herself.

Spaceships.

Clones.

Time travel.

Falling into a volcano.

I could go on. Here's the simple fact: our medium is often *not* based in reality. So as actors, our responses are bigger and more dramatic than they would be in real life. Perhaps the industry doesn't really understand this. If they hired one of us to do a night-time drama or a film, we would make the proper adjustments. We know the difference. I'm happy to tell you that we know what we're doing. We're over-the-top and dramatic for a *reason*.

Still. All that being said, it's frustrating to be categorized in the soap corner. For people to not understand that we can flip that switch. But we deliver what our show requires. It's meant to be an escape. It's fun!

It's daytime TV.

The Hair and me, age 2.

Headshot, age 3.

Imitating a striptease from *Pal Joey*, age 3. (Preparing for my role as Nikki?!)

Taking Suzie for a ride, age 4.

With predator Cosmo Morgan of the
Hollywood Children's Theater, age 8.

Being directed by Alfred Hitchcock in *Marnie*, 1964.

Competing in Junior Stars of America,
the sham beauty pageant.

On the set of *The Beguiled* with (left to right) Clint
Eastwood, Peggy Drier, and Pamelyn Ferdin, 1970.

Being directed by Kirk Douglas in *Posse*, 1974.

On the set of *The Car* with director Elliot Silverstein, 1976.

On the set of *The Fury* with (left to right)
director Brian De Palma, sound technician Ray Quoriz, and Amy Irving, 1977.

Headshot that secured my *Y&R* audition, 1979. (*Courtesy Buddy Rosenberg*)

With *Y&R* costar Steven Ford (Andy Richards), son of President Gerald Ford. (*Courtesy CBS*)

With my *Y&R* makeup man Carlos Yeaggy. (*Courtesy CBS*)

Grandma Jeanne with baby Alex, 1983.

With Alex, eighteen months. (*Courtesy Jonathan Exley*)

My wedding to Edward, 1985.

Baby Elizabeth and Alex. (*Courtesy Kathleen Francour*)

Shots from the 1981 Dick Zimmerman photo session
that changed my image overnight. (*Photographic image Dick Zimmerman*)

Victor (Eric Braeden) and Nikki's first wedding, 1984.
(*Courtesy CBS*)

Christmas party at the Bell's with (left to right) Edward,
Bill, me, Elizabeth, and Alex. (*Courtesy CBS*)

With Dick Clark on the set of *The $25,000 Pyramid*, 1985. (*Courtesy CBS*)

With the spectacular Peter Bergman.
(*Courtesy John Paschal and JPI Studios*)

With Bill and Edward, celebrating an early
milestone, 1997. (*Courtesy CBS*)

With my two husbands, on and off the screen, (left to right) Eric Braeden and Edward Scott. (*Courtesy CBS*)

With *Y&R*'s Bobby Marsino, played by one of my very favorites, John Enos. (*Courtesy Charles Bush*)

With my reel-life other half, the incredible Eric Braeden. (*Courtesy CBS*)

With my idol, Dick Van Dyke, while guesting on his *Diagnosis: Murder* crime drama. (*Courtesy CBS*)

With Aretha at the Emmys, 1999.
Mmmhmmm! (*Courtesy CBS*)

Lunch with Hillary Clinton, 2000.

Attending the 2004 Publicist's Guild Luncheon honoring Clint Eastwood,
where I confessed to stabbing his leg in 1970!

Young Nicholas (Joshua Morrow) with Nikki and Victor
at his first wedding to Sharon, 1996. (*Courtesy CBS*)

With my precious Joshua at my 20th
Y&R anniversary party, 1999. (*Courtesy CBS*)

Joshua will always be my baby boy!
(*Courtesy John Paschal and JPI Studios*)

My darling longtime partner in crime, Doug Davidson (Paul Williams), from 1979 to today.

(Left: Courtesy John Paschal and JPI Studios. Right: Courtesy CBS.)

My other partner in crime, Sharon Case
(Sharon Newman). *(Courtesy Bauer Xcel Media)*

Sharon and Nikki battle it out!

(Courtesy John Paschal and JPI Studios)

Triangle, anyone?
Enter the stunning Eileen Davidson! (*Courtesy CBS*)

With Eric at my 35th *Y&R* celebration, 2014.
(*Courtesy LA Exposures*)

My angel Amelia
and I have so much
fun together!

With husband Edward and daughter Jennifer. (*Courtesy John Paschal and JPI Studios*)

Final touches before our daughter
Jennifer walks down the aisle!

With my daughter, Alex, at my 40th *Y&R*
anniversary party, February 20, 2019. (*Courtesy CBS*)

Me as my idol, Lucille Ball. Transformation and photo courtesy of Karen Faye.

Elizabeth and me. (*Courtesy Charles Bush*)

20

MMMHMM

Being a working actor—shooting nearly every day, the early-morning calls, the hurry up and wait, the fittings, the long hours, studying scripts—feels like a job. Albeit a wonderful one, but for lack of better phrasing, it can start to feel regular. So regular that sometimes we forget that there are people watching. But during a press tour in 1984, I was forced to deal with my new reality.

Eric Braeden and I were flying from city to city, for a publicity junket for CBS. It was specifically organized for the recently aired Nikki and Victor wedding—the first one, of course. Our first appearance was in Dayton, Ohio. I wasn't really expecting much—some interviews, some autographs. We were backstage at the venue when we started hearing them. Cheers, thunderous applause, screaming excitement. *What on Earth?* I stuck my head around the corner to catch a glimpse, and the place was *packed*. Wall to wall. Shoulder to shoulder. I didn't know it at the time, but over eight thousand fans had gathered, waiting to see Nikki and Victor in real life. To see *us*.

I'm not a nervous person. I can't be, doing what I do for a living. If I got nervous about every public appearance, how would I be able to get through anything in my career? But on this day my knees were *knocking*. I thought I'd fall. They introduced us and I literally had to hang on to Eric.

That's when it really hit me. This was no regular job. *The Young and the Restless* was wildly popular!

It did take some learning how to act in public. Trial and error. Sometimes fans approach you at the worst times and it's your job and responsibility (at least in my opinion) to graciously interact. After all, they are the reason you even have a job. But I've made mistakes from time to time. One in particular stands out in my mind.

It was 1980, maybe 1981, way back in the early days after Nikki was first introduced. Before Edward, before Alex, before all of that. I was living in Sherman Oaks and I'd had a long day on the set. I was cranky and tired, but I stopped at the newsstand on my way home, just as I always did. I was gathering the things I needed—my magazines, my newspapers (this was way before news was available with the click of a button; you had to *purchase* news). Anyway, I was flipping through articles, getting ready to pay, and I noticed a woman watching me. I recognized the body language. She was a fan. And she was preparing to approach.

Uggh. I groaned. I simply wasn't in the mood. I normally am! In fact, I enjoy my interactions with fans. But on that particular day, I just wanted to get my magazines and go home.

Sure enough, a minute or so later, there was a tap on my shoulder. I *knew* it was the woman I'd noticed before. I spun around, and yep. It was her.

"Excuse me. Don't you play Nikki on *The Young and the Restless*?" she asked sweetly.

I'm ashamed to say this, but I snapped back.

"Yes, yes, I *do*." This was the very first time I erroneously let a fan know that I really just wasn't up for their adulation.

She got this annoyed look on her face (I don't blame her), extended her hand while holding my gaze, and said, "Nice to meet you. Aretha Franklin."

Oh. My. God. Aretha Franklin! I wanted to rewind that horrible first take and reshoot. I had just bitch-faced the Queen of Soul. Couldn't the earth just open up and swallow me?

I heartily shook her hand while stammering, trying to make it up to her, or apologize as best as I could. "Oh! Oh my! I'm a huge fan! It's a pleasure to meet *you*!" But I just knew it wasn't working. She gave me a big ol' stink eye and went on her way.

Still on the subject of Aretha: Fast forward to 1999, and I was in New York for the Emmys. She was involved with the show that year. All of the photographers saw the two of us on the red carpet, and they said, "Oh, let's get a photo of Mel and Aretha!" So they organize this and get us together, and we're smiling, posing for pictures. Cameras are clicking away. I'm standing there thinking, *Oh god oh god oh god. I hope she does not remember.*

Think again! Through clenched teeth she whispers, "*Mmmhmm.* I still remember you from that night at the newsstand."

I kept apologizing, but oh, well. You know what they say about first impressions. She just waved it off and said, "*Mmmhmm.* Where's Victor? I want my picture made with *him*!"

I remember exactly how she said it: "I want my picture made with Victor." *Made.* So old fashioned, so classy! So queen.

The moral of the story: Treat every fan like they're the Queen of Soul. Thank you for that hard lesson, Aretha. Though I imagine I'll see her in Heaven and she'll say, "*Mmmhmm.* Don't think I forgot about the newsstand."

21

EMOTIONAL MALWARE

I was living the dream. Working on a beloved show. The mother to a *beautiful* baby girl who was my entire heart. The loveliest and most cherished blended family. You would think my life was practically perfect. I'm sure people did! Successful. Financially stable. Famous. I mean, Aretha Franklin stopped me on the street, for crying out loud! But stepping away from the pains of the past isn't easy. I don't imagine those who have suffered childhood abuse walk around lamenting over incidents that happened when they were three or four years old. It would be almost comical to imagine such a scenario.

"How are you?" a friend might ask.

"Oh." They'd pause to heave a heavy sigh. "I was just thinking about 1962. What a rotten year *that* was!"

No, no. For the most part, you find a proper place for the pains of the past. There is a grieving process, and a healing seems to take place. You grow up, go to college, get married—you work hard to establish your career, you might even have children of your own. You live, you laugh, you love. Essentially . . . you move on. But the brain is like a computer, and we are all fully aware that no matter how advanced a computer system might be, it is susceptible to being invaded by a dreadful virus. Childhood trauma functions like this. It is a virus lying dormant in an advanced system. Trauma behaves like a malicious software program ready, at any time, to wreak havoc on the infected organism. Only in this case, the infected organism is poor you. And I'm afraid to say there is no Norton AntiVirus yet available to remove *emotional* malware.

There used to be a great stigma attached to mental illness. You would have been hard-pressed to find people back in the seventies and eighties proudly identifying themselves as mentally ill. So I do love that our society has evolved to one that is working hard to normalize mental illness. I'm happy to play my part. I, Melody Thomas Scott (please, call me Mel), am mentally ill.

My malware goes by the names of Generalized Anxiety Disorder, Panic Disorder, and Agoraphobia. But back when I first started suffering from these, I mostly just thought I was losing my damn mind. Sometimes I think mental illness is the brain's way of yelling at you. It can't speak, so it's got to find some way to let you know it needs help.

There's a particular incident that became the catalyst for me getting the help I needed. Again. I had sought help two or three times previously with no real results. I don't remember what kicked off this particular bout of panic, but when you suffer from anxiety, everything kicks off bouts of panic. Your mind goes from one simple scenario to extremes rather quickly.

Oh, there's a car.

Oh, I'm sure that car could veer over and kill me.

Oh, my God . . . I think it's going to hit me.

Oh, God, I'm going to die.

Oh, please stop . . . I don't want to die.

Somebody please help me, I can't breathe.

If I can't breathe, I will die.

It really happens that way in an anxious mind. Anything and everything is leading to your ultimate demise. You've endured something so terrible that your mind is waiting for the next terrible thing to occur. Constantly. Oftentimes with anxiety, there seems to be no rhyme or reason for the heart palpitations, the inability to breathe, the feeling of suffocation and all-consuming fear. You simply don't understand why you're feeling the way you are.

The incident that led me to seek help yet again occurred when I was at work. I was in the bathroom of my dressing room and terrible anxiety was creeping to the surface. I couldn't breathe, I couldn't even stand. I was lying on the floor in the fetal position. I couldn't stand the feeling of clothes touching my skin in that moment, so I was also naked.

I remember the feeling of despair. The misery that seemed to embody my entire being. I knew I couldn't keep living this way. *No one* would want to live this way. In fact, I wanted to die.

"Mel to the stage," the stage manager's voice boomed through the speakers. Production was ready for me, but I was naked on the bathroom floor in my dressing room. I did want to die. I remember that as one of the lowest points in my entire life. Thoughts of Alex are what ultimately got me up and led me to take the steps I needed to seek out help. I wanted her to have the opportunities I never did. A chance at normalcy. She deserved it. All children deserve it.

The Lifetime network used to produce a series of hour-long biographies called *Intimate Portrait*. Each episode was an in-depth study on a different celebrity. I was featured on one of their episodes back in 2002. The complexities of my mental illness were brought to the forefront on that show. It was the first time I had ever broached the subject publicly. I remember when the episode aired, what got my attention the most was hearing what my co-stars had to say.

None of them had any idea that I was suffering from these disorders.

And it was true. I had told no one. I took great pains. I didn't want people to know how I was living. Mostly because I didn't think they'd understand. How could they? If you don't have anxiety, you can't understand. You can try. You can even be empathetic. But you can't really *know*. In fact, I think it's a knee-jerk reaction to tell the person *to knock it off. Just breathe. You're over-exaggerating.* Believe me, enough people in my life have said these exact words to me. And, I might add, it's infuriating.

During my early years of living with anxiety, there was no medication. If a doctor had said, "Here, try this, Mel. It will help," I would've happily paid top dollar for the prescription. But the proper medication didn't come into my life until the 2000s. Not to say that it wasn't in existence before then, but it was never offered to me.

Medication for anxiety or depression doesn't cure you. Instead, I like to think that it blocks the vicious malware. It quarantines the virus long enough so your brain can realize that it can be OK. It can find another path. Eventually you start to breathe. And the heart rate slows. And the pressure lifts. And you feel hope. A tiny bit of hope is all you really need. Because mental illness can make you feel powerless. It makes you feel victimized, too. *Why am I suffering with this? Why me? Why can't I find a way out?* For me, medication gave me the respite I needed to pull myself out of the all-consuming hole. For me, medication works.

During my years in therapy I've heard the word forgiveness tossed around to assist with healing the mind. In fact, our culture seems quite obsessed with the idea of forgiving. And this idea that forgiving could somehow magically fix me *was* quite intriguing. I read about it. I tried talking to friends and family who seemed like forgiving types. I even looked the word up. Forgiveness? What does that really mean?

for·give /fər'giv/: to grant pardon for or
remission of (an offense, debt, etc.); absolve.

I'll admit, I'm not quite ready to pardon *her.* In fact, if I'm being honest here, it seems like an odd concept when applied to sexual abuse. At least for me. I can attach this idea of absolution to many things, but a parental figure observing and allowing sexual abuse in the hope that they could ultimately benefit from it in some way, shape, or form is unforgiveable to me. I can't grant her pardon for that. I just can't.

Everyone who knows me knows that I'm a spiritual person. Many years ago I had the honor of being read by the world's greatest living medium, George Anderson. He is the gold standard by which all other mediums are measured. We had a wonderful reading. On the phone, no less. At the end of our session he said:

"Someone else is 'in the room.' She's been here since the beginning of our reading. She's finally stepping forward. She says she's your mother, but also your grandmother. Does this make sense to you?"

Oh, boy did it ever. But I hesitated.

"Do you know who I'm speaking of?"

My shock kept me mute.

George then told me her name. I could pretend no more.

"Um, yeah."

"She says she's your grandmother."

George Anderson has an incredible gift.

She came through loud and clear. George said that she realized how hard life was for me under her rule and wanted to apologize and ask my forgiveness.

"Tell her no," I replied seriously. "Tell her she's not forgiven."

"I don't have to tell her. She's hearing you right now."

I thought about that for years afterwards but I didn't change my answer. I've done additional readings with other talented mediums and she continues to come through. Always at the end. Always with the same request. *Forgive me.*

I'm still studying up on it. Still meditating on that word and what it really means to see if I'm even capable of making that decision. But for now, the answer remains. It's not my final answer. But it is my answer for now.

As for my healing and how I've accomplished it, my therapists have played a part. My medication has played a part. My husband has played a part, too. But mostly, it's been my children.

Every now and then something will come up when you're raising a child. I think every parent can relate. Those moments when you question if you're doing the right thing. An issue arises. You think, *what should I do?* Whenever those moments came, I would think back to when I was a child. What would *she* have done? The answer would come to me quickly. I'd just do the exact opposite.

Today my children are such wonderful, lovely human beings. They're so dear to me. I take a little credit for how individually unique and special they are, and it adds to my healing. Their love for me. The love I see them bestow upon their children. There is no greater healing than love. And to see us together is to know love.

Sure there have been bumps along the road. But then you see that they're turning out to be delightful, smart, warm women who are *happy*. You start to realize that you're doing OK. *Look* at them.

And slowly but surely, those pains from the past don't dissolve into nothing, but they lie dormant. Through the years and joys of raising my children, that's where I have found my healing. Life is interesting. It's a school of sorts. I'm always learning. So the best healing? Forgiveness? Hmm . . . If you want. But I say *learn*.

Learn until the day you die.

P.S. George Anderson also told me that one day that I would write a bestselling book. Specifically, a memoir. This was years before I even had the yearning to write one. Could it be the book you're holding right now? I hope so!

22

IT'S A GIRL?

When Edward and I got married, he had a daughter, and so did I. Of course, since our families were blended—and just because, I guess—we wanted to have a child of our own. So once we were married and settled with our two daughters, we decided to try for that illusive boy.

Ten months later I became pregnant.

Telling the show wasn't so daunting this time around. It wasn't like my pregnancy could cause any sort of stir.

I *expected* the usual pregnant actress treatment: large handbags, shots from the bust up, specially placed set pieces. But my expectations never came true. Once more, Bill Bell surprised me with the decision to write the pregnancy into the show. It was such a smart move, and both of those pregnancies drove the ratings. Just as my Alex gave way to Victoria being born on *Y and R*, Lizzie fueled the plotline that gave the Newmans their Nicholas. And those characters are still alive and well on the show today. I love that my real children have a *reel* counterpart!

The scale of the second pregnancy storyline wasn't as big as the first one, but it was similar: Who was the father of Nikki's second baby? Would it be Victor's, yet again, or would it be Jack's?

Like the first time, this baby was proven to be Victor's, thus further cementing their commitment to one another.

Though the gender of the baby on the show was easy to choose and write in, it was not the case with our real-life baby!

We were certain that Elizabeth wasn't an Elizabeth at all, but Michael Julian (that's the original name we had chosen). I should explain. When Lizzie was born December 4, 1988, we were stunned when the doctor declared, "It's a girl!"

I couldn't believe it. We had chosen to not know the gender beforehand. Edward had a daughter, Jennifer. I had Alex. With this pregnancy, we all just *assumed*.

There were also all those old wives' tales about if you're carrying high or low . . . I was carrying low. Apparently that meant boy. Also, Lizzie was huge. She was estimated to be born weighing nine pounds. Apparently that meant boy, too. (She actually weighed in at a bit more than that!) Back then, size was also an indicator of sex. Big babies were boys, period.

I had decorated the nursery in shades of blue, and when my baby shower came around, all of the gifts were for the son I thought I was carrying. Of course, this was the eighties—everything was gendered. And all of our friends were in on the boy theory.

The baby just kept getting bigger and bigger.

I was three weeks past the due date and the doctor finally decided enough was enough. I would have to be induced. It would be birth by appointment. The original date proposed was December 7, but we didn't like that because of Pearl Harbor and the connotations involved with that day. So instead, we chose December 4.

When that day arrived, our entire family and several close friends gathered to make the trek to the hospital with us! Romantic, right? Knowing that only Edward would be allowed in the delivery room, I didn't mind. The more the merrier!

Now, let's just be honest about being induced. It's extremely unpleasant from beginning to end—even with an epidural. But maybe that's because she was so big.

Yes, I said *she*! Despite what everyone thought, we were blessed with yet another girl. Our Elizabeth.

Alex was out in the hallway, asleep, by the time her baby sister was born. But when she woke up, you'd better believe she was thrilled. "I knew I was getting a baby sister," she kept repeating. "I knew it was a girl."

Indeed she had. She was the only one who seemed to know for sure!

But, of course, that led to some practical concerns: I had to change all of the wallpaper in the nursery!

Even though Lizzie turned out to be a girl, Nicholas did not. So I do have a son—fictional or not, Nicholas is my one and only baby boy! And he always will be! Of course, Joshua Morrow (Nicholas) is who I'm really crazy about. He is funny and charming, a wonderful actor. We were so lucky to have cast him. I'll never forget the day that he got the part. He was walking out to the CBS parking lot and I was watching him from the balcony. Suddenly, as if he couldn't contain his joy anymore, he leapt about three feet in the air and let out a very loud "Woohoo!" I probably know better than most of our cast how much *Y and R* can change a young person's life. And he deserves every ounce of happiness. We all adore him.

I digress again!

Raising two children while being a part of the cast of *Y and R* was the best of both worlds. I had the privilege of doing my job, doing what I love most—acting—almost every day. And just as all of our actresses are accommodated, the show allowed my children to be right there with me. I turned my dressing room into a nursery. The nanny would tend to them while I was on the set. But my babies were in my arms when I wasn't on camera. All of this was such a welcome amenity. I know film actresses don't always have it so easy. They're on location halfway around the world. Living out of a trailer all day and night in God knows where. Slugging back and forth from trailer to hotel. Yes, it's been done. Actors do it all the time. But being on *Y and R* and having my children with me, in a comfortable on-set nursery, was like being at home with them. I'm so grateful to CBS for how they accommodate us mothers.

The fans were great during these years as well. Sending me best wishes, cards, baby gifts. All of that was wonderful. I got *thousands* of cards. The whole world was expecting my children along with me. It was one of the most magical times of my life. That era reminds me of how big this show was. It was bigger than life back then.

I should mention Eric Braeden's psychic prediction. We were on the set in the Newman Living Room one day, and I must've been standing twenty feet in front of him. He stared at me for a moment and said, "Darling, are you pregnant?"

And I was! With Lizzie. But I hadn't told anyone yet.

I ran over to him so no one else could hear. "Yes!" I said. "But don't tell anyone! How did you know this?"

He couldn't really say. It was just a feeling, he said.

I wasn't even showing yet. He hasn't had a moment like that since, not with me at least! But who knew Eric Braeden was so prescient?

23

DADDY DEAREST

On *Y and R*, Nikki's mother died in a car accident. And her father . . . well . . . Nikki *killed* him.

But it was an accident!

He was actually the very first person Nikki killed. And she's killed quite a few others since then. The murder of her father happened rather quickly, right after I joined the show. Nikki was living with her father, Nick, and her sister, Casey, in a seedy apartment. Casey moved out because of his sexual advances and tried to warn Nikki that the man was no good. Nikki loved her father and didn't believe her sister. One night Nick attacked her and she picked up a lamp, hit him over the head with it, and he was decidedly dead (being that it was 1979, this action happened off-camera). Of course Nikki was devastated. She never meant to *kill* him. She was only trying to protect herself.

I only bring this up because I find it a rather odd contrast. As Nikki, I killed my father. As Melody Thomas Scott, I saved my father's life. I should probably explain.

My father was a slick confidence man. He was very attractive and extremely charming, with piercing blue eyes that made women swoon.

He was able to talk strangers into doing anything he wanted, and over the years he ripped off a lot of people and destroyed many lives.

Growing up, I rarely saw him. I seldom knew where he lived or if he was even alive. But one night, in 1997, I got this phone call:

"Hello, is this Melody?"

"Yes, it is."

"You don't know me, but I'm your father's girlfriend."

Immediately, alarm bells were chiming. My father? Girlfriend? I knew right away he had attached himself to someone yet again and was most likely sucking her dry. The poor dear. But why was she calling me?

"Your father has had a terrible accident, and he's in a coma in the ICU, down here in Rancho Bernardo. They don't expect him to live through tomorrow. Can you come?"

It was so out of the blue. I hadn't spoken to my father in years. *His girlfriend knew I existed? That I was his daughter? Had my number? And with him ill and on the edge of death, she thought to call me? How bizarre*, I remember thinking.

Her name was Penny. I found out she was a successful business owner. A smart, savvy woman—apparently with a blind spot for love, but we all have our faults. Firmly ensconced in her life, he didn't have to work. He lived in her house and she took care of him. For my father, this was his usual ideal arrangement.

But apparently on this day, my father had been bringing in large bags of sod from the nursery, planning on landscaping the area around her house. He had just carried in one hundred pounds of sod when he collapsed, unconscious. Penny didn't know CPR. She called 911 but by the time the ambulance got there, he'd been deprived of oxygen for too long. He was not expected to live.

I got Penny's info and the name of the hospital, thanked her, and ended the call. That evening I declared something quite bizarre to Edward. "I'm the only person who can save his life," I said.

I didn't know how or why I thought that. We were not close. We barely even knew one another. But I knew. I knew that, if I didn't visit, he would never wake up. So the next morning I drove down to the hospital concentrating on what I knew I had to do upon arrival. Penny was surprised to see me walk in—I'd given no indication the night before as to whether or not I'd be coming.

There he was, in the ICU, hooked up to so many machines. He looked dead. Penny was there, crying, and so was his mother. All the nurses were just standing there waiting for him to pass. It was that close.

I stepped gingerly to the head of the bed, leaned down and whispered in his ear, so that only he could hear me.

"Daddy?" I'd never called him daddy—maybe as a small child, when I didn't know any better.

"Daddy," I repeated, "it's Melody. I'm here. Open your eyes."

His eyes slowly began to flutter. Apparently this is not what coma patients do. I said it again.

The nurses were in disbelief. Machines were beeping that hadn't been beeping before and Penny and his mother were in complete shock. I just kept saying, "Open your eyes. I'm right here, Daddy."

He opened his eyes wide, big and blue, and they locked on mine. Then tears rolled down his cheeks. One of the nurses ran to get the doctor. It was truly unbelievable.

A miracle. I'd gotten him out of his coma, just like I knew I could.

I stayed the night in Rancho Bernardo. I returned home and to work the next day, but I did visit the hospital again. I took Alex the first time, and later, Edward.

Even though he was out of the coma, he was not out of the woods. Because he'd been deprived of oxygen before the ambulance arrived, he suffered permanent brain damage. Not completely debilitating, but holding a conversation would be challenging for him thereafter. After they transferred him to a rehab center, Edward and

I would take the kids every now and then to see him. When I came in, he'd always say, "Hey! There's my kid. Hi, kid."

My father died about seven years after his accident, after my voice brought him impossibly back from the white light. To this day, I'm not sure what my motivation was to save his life. Redemption for Nikki? I jest. Perhaps, deep down, I wanted to prove that I meant something to him.

Yes, I think that was it exactly.

24

ANOTHER GOODBYE

Our family suffered another terrible tragedy that year. Though we weren't together and I was married to Edward, Carlos and I had remained close. He was a wonderful father to Alex and a loving human being.

Carlos and Alex had an excellent father-daughter relationship. Though he was working all the time, often between cities, Carlos saw his daughter every weekend. For a time, he was shooting in New York City, but that didn't stop him—we'd put Alex on a plane from L.A. and Carlos would pick her up in New York. They'd go upstate, hike, or stay in the city. They did it all. I'm happy that my daughter was able to have that sort of relationship with her father—that she has had two amazing male role models in her life.

Every spring break, we took the whole family and close friends to Hawaii. There was always a large group of us and an all-around great time would be had. We all looked forward to those family vacations.

While in Hawaii that year, an urgent call came through from Carlos's good friend, Will, who was staying with Carlos at the time. Unfortunately, the call went through to the kids' room. Alex answered. I'm not entirely sure what transpired on the phone between Alex and Will but the next thing I knew, she came running into my bedroom at 4 a.m. and said, "Mom, you have to talk to Will. He's saying something about my dad and I don't understand."

She was fourteen, but sudden, tragic news like that mixes people's brains up. Alex just couldn't put together what Will was saying.

I got on the phone with him. He'd flown in from New York and let himself into Carlos's condo with his own set of keys. Will had found him in his bedroom. He was long passed, and nothing could've been done to revive him.

I contacted Carlos's mother. She was his only living relative apart from Alex. She lived in L.A., but after learning of her only child's death, was not emotionally able to arrange the funeral. I knew I had to take charge.

The whole pack of us in Hawaii needed emergency airline tickets back to L.A. It wasn't easy, but they were finally secured and we canceled our vacation. A few days after arriving home we learned that sleep apnea was the cause of death, paired with an underlying heart condition. Carlos had not been wearing his CPAP the night he died. CPAP stands for *continuous positive airway pressure*. It's a treatment for sleep apnea. The machine has a hose and mask to deliver constant and steady air pressure while the wearer is asleep.

There was no one else in Carlos's condo the night he died. His CPAP had been tossed aside. That troubles me the most. I still think about it to this day, and wonder: if he had been wearing his CPAP, would he still be with us? I miss him as a friend, and as a father to my daughter. I know Alex misses him, too. At the funeral, which drew hundreds of friends, she presented a beautiful photographic montage to commemorate him and later delivered an incredibly poignant speech at the reception.

It was quite remarkable to see her so poised and determined to let the world know what an amazing man her father had been, and how much she loved him. It's important to mention that when Alex's father died, her behavior completely transformed. Before Carlos's passing, Alex had suffered with ADD and, despite her intelligence, *struggled* through school. In elementary school she could be quite a handful. She was always very smart, but with the complexities of her ADD the teachers had a difficult time getting her to follow rules and acquiesce to the structure of their classrooms.

One year Alex was getting into so much mischief that her teacher, Mrs. Seltzer, contacted me and we came up with a plan—a standing appointment every single Wednesday after school. Both Edward and I always attended. We thought that if she knew we had this appointment, it might help her to straighten out. But it didn't. I remember one Wednesday afternoon, sitting at a children's desk across from Edward, who was sitting at another. The teacher was giving us a detailed report regarding some of the shenanigans Alex had been up to that past week. Though I tried to always remain calm at these teacher meetings, I was unexpectedly reduced to tears. I started crying right there in the classroom. Mrs. Seltzer looked at me and placed her hand gently on my arm.

"Don't cry, Mrs. Scott. It will be all right."

She was right. It would be all right. But it would take time to get there. We faced a long haul of worry. We did everything to seek out help. First we tried biofeedback, which was a very expensive, non-drug therapy that uses sensors placed on your head to help you gain control over body processes like heart rate, blood pressure, etc. Several weeks of Alex being hooked up to sensors didn't yield any results. Highly recommended therapists didn't work, either. We tried so many things back in those days—any alternative to Ritalin. Ritalin had received so much bad press and there was such a stigma attached to parents who were putting their children on medication, but we came to a point where we felt we had exhausted all other options.

We did end up trying the medication. Ritalin worked. For Alex, anyway. We saw a difference right away. But after her father's death,

Alex suddenly started getting straight A's. She no longer needed Ritalin and school became comparatively easy. Alex made a complete 180. She worked hard in her junior and senior years to get good grades and was a star athlete. After graduating, she went off to new adventures at UC Berkeley.

Alex and her father were always close, and he would've done anything for her—I know that. I like to imagine that his first order of business on the other side was helping Alex. Not that she needed it. She was finally succeeding in her studies on her own merit. But I know that he will always be by her side, running defense, her most special guardian angel.

PART III

★

NIKKI
NEWMAN

25

A FEW OF
MY FAVORITE THINGS

Being on a daytime drama is very different than working on a film or even a serialized primetime drama. When you're on a soap, especially for forty years, you have so *many* storylines that it is impossible to remember them all. Though some have stood out as personal favorites.

Very early on there was a character named Edward who developed a crush on Nikki while she was stripping at The Bayou, and he started stalking her. Nikki was so naïve, she had no idea that she was in danger. The actor playing him, Paul Tulley, was phenomenal. Such a sweet guy in real life . . . but boy, he played crazy and menacing and *threatening* so well. It was like nothing I'd seen before. That red light on the camera would go on, and he'd look at me—I was literally terrified. I shed hundreds of tears during that storyline!

The character Edward always said, "Oh, Nikki. I can't wait to bring you home to meet my mother."

Eventually it came to be that he actually did bring Nikki home. Only his mother was long dead and her ashes were in an urn on the mantel. *Very* Norman Bates.

Another storyline that I loved was the one that revolved around the New World cult. Back when this storyline was airing in the early eighties, talk of cults wasn't common. When I found out Nikki was going to be a cult member, I bought several books on the subject so that I could understand the cult mindset, and how it was even possible to succumb to such brainwashing. My research led me to learn that Nikki was the perfect victim for a cult. Cults attract insecure, fearful, "nobody likes or wants me," "I'll always be the little guy," "I'm not important" kinds of people. And at that time in her life, Nikki was all of those things. So the storyline was very appropriate. I became fascinated with the pathology of both sides: the leader and the follower.

The climax of that storyline ended with the cult being engulfed in flames. We had fire officials on the set to ensure everyone's safety. They were the experts. I had my notes from the director and my notes from the fire safety crew. Whenever there is a stunt, gun, or explosion, fire, etc., required for a scene, the stuntman/safety expert's directions supersede your director's commands. This is a SAG/AFTRA (actor's union) rule.

I remember that we rehearsed the blocking of the scene many times before going to tape.

"After this line of dialogue, you girls walk to your final mark, and you stand precisely there. Don't stand to the left; don't stand to the right, because there's going to be fire here, here, and here," one of the safety officials would explain for the tenth time. "The director plans to cut to you for your reactions, so please be on your marks. Don't worry. Fire won't be on you, it won't be near you. You have to go to these *exact* marks. Got it?"

I nodded. "Ok. Got it." The actress with me nodded too. We were ready.

So now we are shooting, and they cue the fire, and within three seconds she and I looked at each other and got the hell out of there.

Forget our marks! We ran for our lives. The heat was so intense. They'd misjudged just how hot it would be. So when the camera panned over to us, we were *gone*! I remember that vividly because, when your life is in danger, you don't hit your mark. You run. If you think you're going to die, don't be professional!

When I think of fire on the set, I flash forward to when the original Newman Ranch burned down, which we still mourn—and a lot of the fans still mourn. I will never understand why they chose to do that.

Again, there was a big, controlled fire on the set. I wasn't in the scenes, only the phenomenal Sharon Case. Her character goes a little crazy and sets fire to the Newman Ranch. I just remember walking around the set, taking pictures of one of the darkest days of my life, of Nikki's life, of *Y and R*. I just thought, this is so *wrong*. I was taking pictures and crying that *this was actually happening*. It was a crushing blow to a lot of us. It certainly was to Eric and me.

That was like my house. Not my own real-life house, but my house all the same. That's one of the ways an actor's mind goes beyond a non-actor's mind, in that when I was in that set, I was the mistress of that house in my mind. If the prop crew had not set things exactly right, I would say, "Wait a minute! Where's the porcelain pig that's normally on this side table?" or, "This doesn't feel right, something is out of place." It was difficult because for so many years, for so many *decades*, that was my house. They burned it down, and it was just devastating to me. This was many years ago—two regimes ago— and I'm still not over it.

If you're curious to know how they did this, well, that's a fair question. I guess it would have been kind of impressive if it hadn't been so upsetting. I think back to that cult plot, when I had to bail my final mark to escape that horrific heat. Cut to decades later: they had fire experts come in again to run piping behind the sets, or wherever they wanted to see fire. But this time I was watching them *destroy my house*. In front of me.

When explaining how I try to make a scene believable, I have always said, "I just move into Nikki in my mind." But that day I took it very personally. Eric did as well. But he wasn't walking around the set crying.

Most actors don't live in the same set for decades like I did. It's usually, "Oh, you have this for two weeks and it's over." But this set was mine. It wasn't my home—I knew that—but it was the home of a huge part of my life. I knew it as part of my *normal*, as it were, and that made it so meaningful. I knew it like I knew Nikki. And then, in a blaze of glory, it was gone.

Okay, this topic is too upsetting. Still. Let's move on . . .

Another all-time favorite of mine is the backstory of Victor Newman. Fans discovered that Victor, a man richer than God, was actually given up by his poor young mother and raised in an orphanage. Nikki decides, after discovering the truth of Victor's upbringing, that for a Christmas gift she's going to find his birth mother. The great actress Dorothy McGuire was cast in the role. That storyline enabled the audience to see a softer side to Victor for the first time, which made him an even more complex character. No longer was he simply rich and powerful. The opportunity to show vulnerability gave him even more substance. That was such an important ingredient for the complexity of Victor Newman. In fact, Eric was close to leaving the show before that happened. He didn't like playing just one note over and over. That storyline twist gave him the layers he needed to enjoy being Victor.

Another favorite was when I became pregnant and Bill Bell decided to write it into Nikki's storyline. Nikki was unwed and pregnant, and involved with two different men. It created a dramatic story that the fans loved. Who was the father of Nikki's baby? Is it Kevin or is it Victor? This story was extremely popular with the fans. And, of course, it did turn out to be Victor's daughter, Victoria.

Shortly after that story arc, Victor, Nikki, and Ashley started a many-years-long love triangle. Victor started having an affair with Ashley, which made for huge stories and huge ratings. I loved it, because Eileen Davidson, who plays Ashley, was so good and so very different from Nikki. She was cool, sophisticated, worldly—the total opposite of Nikki. So there Victor was, in the middle of these two women who couldn't be more different, deeply in love with both of them.

We shot on location for one of those episodes, which is always exciting and not something we do anymore. We flew up to Carmel and shot the exteriors, all on horseback, for the scenes. Those were the days . . .

I can't talk about favorite episodes without mentioning the drinking. I have made it no secret that I love it when Nikki falls off the wagon, and her drinking has been woven through so many of her storylines. It's just so much fun! As the fans say, there's no Nikki like a drunk Nikki! It's a tragic, yet amusing way of playing her and gives me another layer that I can add to her emotional make-up.

Usually, the writers will bring another actor in to play opposite Nikki in her alcoholic haze, and that character is most often a drinker, too. Always so much fun! Much lighter than our traditional dramatic heaviness. It's such an interesting dichotomy that Nikki, who has everything—wealth, family, home, fame, and marriage, and is the toast of the town—can still sink so low. If that can happen to Nikki Newman, it can happen to anyone. For people who struggle with alcoholism it shows how random the humanity of addiction can sometimes be.

Another fun scenario is when Nikki gets into a fight. Specifically a catfight. And if it's with Sharon, even better! Sharon and Nikki have always been on the outs more often than not. And the fans *love* it. Sharon Case and I love it, too! I believe their very first fight was when Sharon roped Nikki into climbing down to the sewers to find a body whose death Sharon was incriminated in. When we shot those scenes, production hired live rats to run along the pipes in that dingy sewer! Don't hate me, but I'm afraid I'm not fond of rats. Even though these were trained, and accompanied by human rat wranglers, I didn't trust one of them not to bite Sharon or me if we caught them off-guard. Thankfully, none did, and Sharon and I had the best time shooting those scenes together! Part of the fun was the constant verbal barbs we were throwing at each other. This was an element that had not been included in our previous bouts. Adding those insults to our already contentious scenes brought the fans more enjoyment than ever, and they've begged for Sharon/Nikki catfights ever since. They can't get enough. Neither can Sharon and I!

Back in the earlier days, Nikki often fought with the character Diane Jenkins. In fact, Nikki ended up killing Diane. Which might make you think, *shouldn't Nikki be in prison?* Well, she *was*. She's been in prison. She's been in jail. But she always gets off on a technicality, or through the power of the Newman family. You can't keep a character incarcerated very long on a soap because it takes them off the canvas of the show for too long. So Nikki was in and out of prison fairly quickly. In the alternate reality of soap operas, you *can* get away with murder.

Of course some of my most favorite storylines are those that involved Nikki Reed becoming Nikki *Newman*.

As I have mentioned, initially, both Eric and I were confused about our pairing. I'm sure my brows furrowed in puzzlement when the scripts hinting at us getting together were delivered to my house. Eric and I both wondered what Bill was thinking. But as I said earlier, Bill could be very psychic about these things. I don't know what it was that he saw in us, but in retrospect it's clear that he saw *something*.

Essentially, we became a daytime TV super-couple. The super-couple moniker is an interesting animal. Though we are all *Y and R* stars in our own right, Eric and I know that the fans want to see us *together*. The press does, too. Everyone's ultimate goal, as far as *Y and R* is concerned, is to have the two of us in the same frame, in the same news article, on the same cover. So we've ended up spending a lifetime together! On and off camera. Over the years, we have been blessed with becoming one of the most enduring super-couples in daytime television history. Certainly in television as a whole.

It helps that Eric and I get along. I like to keep things fun between us by playing pranks on him from time to time. Perhaps this is yet another clue as to why he calls me obstreperous! One particular prank comes to mind—nothing as awful as stabbing Clint Eastwood though, thank goodness. Edward and I were in Hawaii on vacation. Just the two of us, this time. I don't remember which island we were on, but we heard from our hotel's concierge that Eric Braeden was doing a personal appearance in Maui, a short boat ride from where we were staying. I thought about the coincidence of Eric and I being so far from our usual playground, yet relatively close in islands, and couldn't resist doing *something about it!* I said to Edward, "Why don't we take a boat tomorrow and surprise Eric!" Edward was game.

So I dreamt up my plan of action. I decided to dress up as the goofiest fan ever. I somehow located a pair of denim overalls. I put my hair in braids, wore a straw hat, drew freckles on my cheeks with an eyebrow pencil, and blacked out a couple of my teeth. We hopped on a boat, arrived on Maui, and hailed a taxi, heading to the Sears where he was appearing. This was a long time ago, so security was nothing like what it would be today. It was much more lax back then. So I walked into the Sears and found the site of his appearance as it was coming to a close. Again, not one security guard stopped me! I climbed over the stanchions and ran right up to Eric, looking like something straight out of *The Beverly Hillbillies*. I put on a kooky accent, and said, "Oh, Victor! I'm yer biggest fan! I sures am!"

Talk about being out of context . . . He didn't recognize me at all! I carried on and on. He was trying to be polite but I could tell he was thinking, *This fan is completely out of her mind. Someone save me*! But then my accent slipped and my real voice came out and I saw the recognition in his eyes.

"Mel?" he exclaimed.

Ha! The jig was up. I took off my straw hat and hugged him. We had such a great laugh about that. This is the core of us. We are good friends who love to laugh. It adds to our unique chemistry. Yet I think back to the very early courtship of Victor and Nikki, when Eric and I barely knew each other, and our chemistry was through the roof! Ah, it is an elusive, indefinable curiosity, this chemistry stuff . . .

Another time, back in 1996, Eric and I were chosen by the Academy to host the Daytime Emmys. That was so exciting for the both of us. We flew to New York, got down to the business at hand, and the whole thing felt larger than life. From the fittings, hair and makeup, to traveling from midtown to uptown to downtown for interviews—it was a lot. When you're hosting *anything* live, there's just so much pressure. But Eric is and always has been my rock.

The evening of the broadcast arrived. Waiting in our respective wings of Radio City Music Hall, we reviewed all of our rehearsals, but . . . I did mention this was live, right? There is no "back to one, let's take it again." Eric was to enter on stage right, I was to enter on stage left, and we each had our own staircase to descend. I was in a floor-length, beaded Badgley Mischka gown and six-inch heels. And there were no handrails.

You don't want to fall down the stairs on live television. I remember asking the stage manager, during rehearsal, how many stairs there were.

"Uh . . ." He scratched his head. "Maybe thirty?"

I knew I wouldn't be able to hold onto Eric like I had in Ohio all those years ago. We wouldn't even meet until we both walked downstage to the microphone. As the live show began and our names were introduced, the SRO audience was on its feet, screaming. Screaming so loud that I almost missed my cue! I drew in a breath, steeled myself, and silently counted my way down those stairs. I made it to the bottom, still upright. Almost home free, I started to walk the few steps to the microphone. It was only then that I realized my knees were uncontrollably knocking together, just like in Dayton, Ohio. My biggest concern was whether the live and television audiences would be able to see my gown quivering from all that knee action. Thankfully, they settled down quickly. The rest of the show went off without a hitch and I enjoyed every minute of it! What an exhilarating, unbelievable experience that was.

Another time, Eric and I were in Milan, Italy, to accept individual Telegattos for our work on *Y and R*. A Telegatto is a very prestigious award. The live telecast was over five hours long. All in Italian. By the time our awards came along we were blurry-eyed. Eric speaks German, Spanish, and French, but not Italian. On stage, Eric gracefully delivered a *grazie*. But unbeknownst to him, I had learned a rather lengthy acceptance speech, in Italian, phonetically. The audience members weren't the only ones who were surprised. Eric couldn't believe it. That process helped me years later when, at Eric's thirty-fifth *Y and R* anniversary celebration, I gave another speech—in German! I knew I had to go the extra mile for him. His eyes filled with tears listening to my speech. Afterwards the press wanted to know what I'd said! Eric only smiled and told them it was a secret message meant only for him.

I do think Bill Bell had *My Fair Lady* in mind when he put the wealthiest man in the world together with this uncultured, poor, young stripper. Part of Victor's attraction for Nikki wasn't just that he thought she was adorable, but that he thought he could mold her into a proper lady. I think with being very rich and successful comes a unique kind of boredom. Nikki *excited* him. She presented a big challenge at a time in his life when he really needed one. Which makes for such good story, especially when Nikki is confronted with someone like Sharon Newman (played by the amazing Sharon Case) throwing her stripper past into her face, reminding her exactly where she comes from.

The incomparable Jess Walton (Jill) can never resist needling Nikki, either. Some people in Genoa City used to enjoy reminding Nikki that she would never be a *real* Newman. The thought that Nikki would never fully be accepted by her peers was a frustrating situation for Nikki, but it drove her as well. I think I can now safely say that she has finally gained the town's respect and, Lord knows, she's certainly earned it.

Another fun moment happened not that long ago. We had a scene in Victoria's Living Room in which the family had gathered to celebrate one of the grandchildren's birthdays. It was scripted that Nikki was to come to the door holding a gift bag. We ended up having to do the scene three or four times for whatever reason. When your scene has to be reshot a few times and you are carrying something, the prop wranglers come and reset that for you.

I don't know what happened that day, but after the third or fourth take, I realized—uh oh, the gift bag I'm supposed to have in my hand is still on the coffee table from the prior take! Anyone else would've just yelled cut. Actors do it all the time. But instead I decided to go downstage, get down on all fours, and *crawl* into the set, making sure I stayed below the camera frame. The actors on the set were *shooting*, and they could see me doing this. My heart and soul, Amelia Heinle (who plays Victoria), will never let me forget it! They all saw me scurrying across the floor like a hermit crab, challenging their concentration. I remember poor Amelia trying so hard not to focus on what I was doing. But there I was, slithering across the floor. I finally made it to the table, grabbed the gift bag, and crawled back out, arriving at the door just in time for my cue! Sure, I could've said, "Cut!

I need my bag!" but where's the fun in that? It also shows how good our actors are since they never broke their concentration. I'm sure they just thought, "Oh, there's Mel, doing something crazy again."

They're very used to me by now.

I can't leave the wedding extravaganza off the list of favorites—Victor and Nikki's first wedding, of course. They'd be divorced four years later, then remarried ten years after that. But the fans had waited in eager anticipation for that *first* wedding. So had we. It was one of the most elaborate and expensive weddings daytime TV had ever seen. An outside fashion-designing team (Jeran) was hired to make my dress, which ended up weighing thirty-five pounds with all the yards of silk and bling it had attached to it (after the wedding was shot, the dress itself went on tour across the country as a wedding fashion epic!). There were many former cast members invited back for the wedding, which was wonderful. It took place at the Colonnade Room, where Nikki walked down its grand spiral staircase. Elegant and beautiful. Classic *Y and R*.

The episode even started with Nikki looking into her mirror that morning and saying, "It's my wedding day" to no one in particular. This was signature Bill Bell. He had all his brides say this exact same thing on the morning of their weddings until he retired. Even after that, when protégés of Bill took over, our brides still said it!

The actual day of the wedding was a long and difficult shooting day, more so for me as the dress was so heavy. Its two designers were at my side constantly fussing and fixing and making adjustments to it. By late afternoon I was actually lying on the soundstage floor for our union-required five-minute breaks. The designers were beside themselves at seeing their baby on the floor (the dress, not me), but I couldn't help it. Dragging around that dress all day was exhausting. I'll never forget the shot where Victor picks up Nikki (and her dress) in his arms and sweeps her up the stairs. I was concerned about how much would be seen in that action, so I had a pair of men's cotton polka dot underwear on underneath that stunning gown. Eagle-eyed fans can catch a glimpse of the underwear in the episode!

I also can't talk about favorites without mentioning some of the not-so-favorites. And I'm just going to be honest here. Over the years there have been a few dreadful storylines that I absolutely abhorred.

When Nikki ran for State Senate. *Oh*. I groan in agony just thinking of it. I mean, politics? In my opinion, that's not a story that viewers want to tune in for. Let's face it—it's boring. All this political mumbo jumbo, debates, and campaigning. It's not for soaps. People don't even want to deal with it in *real* life. And Nikki, of all people. Nikki! What does she know about the political world? I mean, she's at home arranging flowers and serving tea, and then the writers force her to say, "I want to run for State Senate." Curious at best.

I hated every bit of it—every script, every word. I was so relieved when it was over. I don't remember the brainchild behind that one, but I don't think I've hated another storyline that much. Ever.

Soon after that, there was another storyline that people referred to as Clear Springs. I refer to it as a whole lot of nothing. There was some building in Genoa City that had collapsed. People were trapped inside. Were they alive? How could we get them out? It went on for so long that I don't think anyone cared if the people got out alive or not.

But I don't think any other storyline over my entire forty-year run on the show has made me as sad as when Cassie died. Nikki's son, Nicholas, marries Sharon, and they end up raising her child, Cassie. Cassie was played by Camryn Grimes, who came to us when she was just seven years old. An amazing young actress who was very popular with the fans, but for some reason the writers decided to have Cassie die in a car accident. Nikki and Victor were like this child's grandparents. On set and off, everyone adored her. We could not believe that she was being forced to leave the show. When we shot those final hospital scenes, none of us were acting. We were shedding our own tears. It was very upsetting for all of us. Years later, she's back playing Mariah, Cassie's twin sister. And it is so great to have her back! But we were gut-wrenched having to endure that storyline of a young girl we loved taking her last breath.

That utter heartache aside, I also tend to dislike when the writers put our characters into costumes for Halloween or a masquerade ball. It never works. The last time they did that, I was Mae West. I mean, *why*? Mae West? The viewers don't even know who she is. And the witticisms they made me say, they were just so out of date.

Many years prior there was a masquerade ball, and they made Nikki a phantom. Black tights, black robe, a cape, and a mask. And please, don't take a character you want people to tune in to watch and put a mask on them. To this day, I don't understand the decision. The phantom of what? The opera? It didn't help that Victor was something totally unrelated. Our costumes clashed in an almost comical way.

My opinion is that if you're going to have an established character wear a costume, ask their portrayer what they would like to be. That would avoid the ill-at-ease performances that we have suffered in the past. And I certainly count myself in that mix. Just because so-and-so plays a great so-and-so, doesn't mean he or she would make a terrific [insert any Halloween character here]. If I am ever asked, I would say that I want to be Lucille Ball! Lucy Ricardo will *never* be out of style! One year I actually went as Lucy to Heather Tom's (the first actress who played adult Victoria) costume party. It was amazing. Karen Faye, my dear friend and hair/makeup artist-extraordinaire of forty years, did my makeup to look exactly like Lucy. Hair, too. And since I just mentioned hair. Oh, let's talk about *that* . . .

26

HAIR!

I've always thought of my hair as rather problematic, and today, I still do. Even as a child, when I had long hair hanging past my waist, it made me stand out and I just didn't like that. Most kids want to blend in when they're little. I was so unlike my friends in so many other ways, and nobody else had bleached hair. So why me? When I did *The Beguiled* when I was thirteen, they dyed my hair a rusty red. I wasn't fond of that look either.

It's one of those things that's said about me so often; I suppose I've just come to accept it. Like, "Oh, she's such a wonderful actress, and her *hair!*" My hair is always a topic of discussion. In my dressing room at work, I still have many magazine covers framed on the wall. Any new person who comes in can't even talk to me for a few minutes because they're busy looking at all the hairdos. My cavalcade of hairdos. They're not even covers anymore, just hair!

Most women think I'm so lucky to have such thick, resilient hair. But it's not a blessing. Not to me. I've always wanted it to be thinner and straighter. Its natural state is coarse, wavy (and not a pretty wave), way too thick . . . a completely unruly head of hair. With a mind of its own. I can't just hop out of the shower and go. Not if I just washed my hair. Air drying would take all day. A blow dryer? An hour or more. Who has that kind of time? In fact, I'm always allotted *more* time in hair (and makeup) to allow for the extra time and effort it takes to wrangle. It's absurd. Perhaps my hair needs its own billing in the credits.

I've always thought thinner hair would be easier to manage. My reasoning? You can make thinner hair look bigger, but you can't make thick hair look smaller. And trust me, I get the whole grass-is-always-greener thing. Maybe with thin hair I'd long for my thick, coarse, not-so-easy-to-maintain hair. But I don't think so! Still, everyone seems to think I'm so fortunate.

If I'm not at work and don't have to look presentable, I do *nothing* with my hair and it looks however *it* wants to. I only wrestle with it when I have to. It likes to take the weekends off.

And, I'm married to a man who is *obsessed* with hair. If he doesn't like the way I'm wearing it, he'll suggest a change. He's actually got alternative styles in mind. I swear the man must've been a hairdresser in a past life. When he was our producer on *Y and R*, I would come down to the stage to shoot my scenes, and if he didn't like my hair, the same request would be made. Maddening! And it wasn't just me. It could happen to any actor on the show! "We're moving on to the next set of scenes [insert any actress's name here], go change your hair."

The thing with Edward—and most men—is that they don't understand hair terminology, or salon-speak. Even today, in comparing notes with CBS hairdressers, we'll laugh about how when Edward doesn't like someone's hair. He'll go to the stylist and say, "You know, her hair is kind of, unh, and I want it to be more, ah!" He will let his hands do most of the talking in an as-yet-not-identified language.

When I was his target, my hairdressers would respond to him, "Ahh. OK," as they met my eyes in the mirror and desperately prayed for a translator.

Since we're on the subject of hair, I simply must bring up Victoria Rowell. Vickie is a wonderful actress and was a part of the *Y and R* family for many years playing the role of Drucilla Winters. I feel I should take this moment to explain a few of the things she's spoken to the press about concerning me. The most offensive situation started off with an angry tirade about hair. Fake hair. A clown wig to be specific.

The incident revolved around a carnival. Our set designers created a real carnival on one of the stages for a few episodes. Though I didn't have any scenes in that set, I *was* working that day and a lot of us idle-at-the-moment actors thought we would have fun with this out-of-the-ordinary set. A few of us, along with some of the hair and makeup team, were standing near one of the prop carts, which had a bunch of clown wigs stuffed into a bin. So we decided to put them on. Just giggling, pretending to be clowns. It was all very silly. We were behind the scenes, *making* a scene. No harm, no foul.

Out of nowhere, Victoria Rowell was upon us. She took one look at me in the wig and started carrying on in a forceful manner; I couldn't even grasp what she was saying.

"I'm sorry? What?" I was totally confused.

She thought I was making a statement about *her* hair because of the multi-colored Afro wig I was wearing, and accused me of being a racist because of it.

And there you have it.

27

I'LL NEVER FORGIVE O.J.

O.J. Simpson nearly *ruined* daytime television.

I don't think anyone could have predicted how wildly popular daytime dramas would become, or that *The Young and the Restless* would be television's *number one* daytime drama with millions of fans escaping into the town of Genoa City. (I've been to the real Genoa City—it actually exists. In Wisconsin.) But today, I think it's fair to say that daytime drama isn't what it used to be. Literally. In the nineties, there were well over a dozen different daytime dramas on the air. To name a few:

All My Children
Another World
As the World Turns
General Hospital
Guiding Light
One Life to Live

Don't get me wrong. *The Young and the Restless* is still the highest-rated daytime drama on television and has been for over thirty years. We're still going strong. In fact, I'm still keeping my jaded

fingers crossed that I'll get to play Nikki's evil twin and wreak absolute *havoc* on her life. Back in the nineties, soaps were what almost
everyone was watching. But after a time, things took a turn, and it all
goes back to O.J. Simpson.

On June 17, 1994, I have written in my day planner: O.J. runs.

I distinctly remember staring at the TV screen in my kitchen,
mesmerized by that white Bronco as it made its way down the 405
freeway. The entire world was watching O.J. When the decision
came down that his trial would be televised, fans switched the channel from their imaginary dramas to a real-life one. Though a lot of
people had VCRs to tape their soaps each day, those viewings were
not counted by the Nielsen ratings folks. For the latest on O.J. they
tuned into CNN, Headline News, Court TV . . . any network that was
airing the trial and its attendant commentary. They were hungry for
the details. This was the beginning of a new era of television. The
very first televised, celebrity court trial. It didn't matter what they
usually watched—from that very first court day, they were now
watching O.J. That's right: For 134 days, the trial of O.J. Simpson
was carried out on live, daytime television.

But guess what else played out on daytime television? If you
guessed soap operas, you'd be correct. We didn't think anything of
it, at first. After all, everyone was watching the trial—including all of
the actors of our show. We were all human, after all. And, as we and
the world were glued to our TV screens, something else began to
happen: our ratings started to slowly decline. We'd been going
steadily for so long that it didn't really mean anything at the time.
During the early days of the trial, reporters would ask me or Eric or
anyone else, "Do you think this will change things?" "Of course
not!" we all answered. And that was the truth. We didn't think it
would change anything, at least not permanently. I don't think any
of us saw *how* it could change things. The trial would end, someday,
and the viewers would come back.

But the O.J. trial created such a loss in viewership for every single daytime show that it had a major, lasting impact. It was such a decline that, to this day, soaps have never recovered. And we just did not see it coming. Here's what we didn't account for, I think: people lost the routine of it all. What's that saying—it takes thirty days to make a habit and one day to break it? That's how it went. People who'd been watching the show for many years stopped to watch the O.J. trial, and when it concluded they just didn't come back. Their habit had been broken.

Well, the O.J. trial was the trial of the century. *Eleven* months long. That's eleven habits made and broken—or one habit broken eleven times, in our case. Can you imagine? People tuned in every single day. It's funny—we were part of the problem. *We* were all watching the trial, too. It really just swept up the whole world. But oh, did it have a negative impact for us. People got out of the habit of daytime television and into the habit of *news*. This also ushered in a new era of *reality* television. People now yearned for a different type of drama. A real-life drama. Daytime television hasn't been the same since.

28

FLOAT LIKE A BUTTERFLY

I love interacting with fans. I enjoy the opportunity to hear how they feel about storylines, the writing, etc., directly from their mouths. It's one of my favorite things to do (though Aretha Franklin might not believe me!).

Something that really changed my view of the show happened in 1996. As I've said, Bill and Lee Bell lived in Chicago for most of the early years of the show. They also had a beautiful lakeside home on Lake Geneva, Wisconsin. They knew this part of the Midwest very well.

During the summer of 1996, they invited me, Eric, Tracey Bregman (Lauren Fenmore), Kimberlin Brown (Sheila Carter), and our respective spouses to take part in an event at an adjacent estate, which had originally been a Playboy Mansion but was now an elegant hotel compound.

The day after the event, Bill told us he and Lee were taking us on a little adventure to surprise us. Well, none of us could guess what it was. We weren't expecting what actually happened. Bill drove us straight to this tiny, one-horse town. Just as we began to wonder where we were, he announced, "This is Genoa City. The *real* Genoa City."

As you can imagine, we were thrilled—and very surprised! The real-life Genoa City was nothing like our TV version. For one thing, the locals say Gen-*O*-a rather than GEN-*oa*.

And best of all? I'm pretty sure, from what I saw, that every resident watches our show with pride.

We went all around, checking out stores, walking through the streets. It wasn't like there was that much to see but we were all just so excited to be seeing it. On one corner we spotted a bank, and I had an idea (Ethel, I've got another idea!).

Looking in through the windows, I could see behind the bank counter that there were lots of tellers lined up, all women. (Being a tiny town, progress takes a little longer!) I assumed that they, like everyone else in town, probably watched our show.

I roped Eric into another plot and decided to play a little prank. No one knew we were in town. I put Eric into position outside of one of the bank's windows, but I kept out of sight. One of the tellers noticed him, and excitedly turned to the teller next to her, but as soon as she did, I would pull Eric out of sight. And I kept doing that! As soon as they'd look away, I pushed Eric in, and when they looked up, I'd pull him out of view.

Finally, they realized what was happening, and they all came out on the sidewalk to meet him. Victor and Nikki in real-life Genoa City! I'm sure they've never forgotten it! I know I haven't.

I can think of another instance that was especially meaningful to me: I went to Oklahoma City right after the bombing—I was part of a group of celebrities that were flown to OK City to visit the victims in hospitals. I think it was the first time that I could see how very much we mean to people who are hurting and in need. Many had suffered excruciating injuries, many couldn't speak. When we would walk in, it lifted their spirits. That meant so much to me. And I wasn't expecting it—after someone's been in such a horrific event like that, to put a smile on their face. The human spirit is mighty indeed.

Sometimes people think that when we celebrities are interacting with fans it doesn't mean much to us. That we're simply filling a role or playing a part. Not true! In fact, Elizabeth's godparents are some of our closest friends. Bob and Bonnie Caudle. We met them as fans. They invited us to their small town, Roanoke Rapids, North Carolina, to take part in an American Cancer Society benefit, and we got to know each other. The husbands got along great, we wives got along great, and they had children close in age to ours. Over the years we became like family. And when Elizabeth was born, we named them her godparents.

I think that the fans are always interested in hearing those stories because they don't think that something like that could ever happen. But there is something to be said for being authentically you. Our families are still close to this day. We fly across the country to see each other. We don't really remember that we met them as fans. Just when we start to forget, someone will ask how we met, and we have to remind ourselves—well, yes, they were *fans*.

Speaking of fans—they're *everything*. Without them, we wouldn't even be on the air. I've always been diligent about responding to my fan mail. Now, with social media, it's easier to get information out to many people all at once, but a lot of people still appreciate snail mail. Our *Y and R* fans deserve it. They are extremely loyal, so loving and supportive. The gifts they sent for the births of my children are a perfect example of their kindness and generosity. I'm very grateful, and it remains important to me to have a genuine relationship with them as a way to say thank you for what they've given us. A career. A family. A wonderful life.

I joined Twitter in 2009, not having a clue what I was doing! The fans were so helpful. They tweeted to me about how to navigate this new animal. I'd tweet, *"Hey guys, I'm here and I don't know what to do! How does this work?!"* And they would tell me. Encouraging me all the way. I love to interact with my fans. Especially if they have something meaningful to say that stands out, *or* if I find them funny.

My BFF Claudine? We *met* on Twitter. People thought, *you're crazy*, and yes, I am, but so is my precious Claudine! She is the yin to my yang and we have become very close. She and I have the same brain, the same sense of humor. Thanks, Twitter!

You can glean some interesting information from tweets. You can see what people like, what they think is funny. And maybe you might start to think, hey, we have a lot of things in common. That's what happened with Claudine and me. After communicating back and forth on Twitter for so long, we finally met one year when she attended the Emmys as a guest and it was like we had known each other forever. We made an instant real-life connection. It's been one of those very rare, once-in-a-lifetime friendships that you don't find very often.

There's a well-known television festival hosted in Monte Carlo, Monaco, every year. Edward and I have been invited a few times and they definitely pull out all the stops. Dinner with royalty, red carpets, private drivers, gorgeous hotel rooms, constant hair and wardrobe changes. We ladies have to change so often—everything is documented by the stylists!

During our first visit we were seated at Prince Albert's table for a royal dinner. I was seated directly next to him and I suddenly worried about how to proceed. What was I supposed to say to a *prince*? He was so poised and . . . princely.

But as we made our way through the first course, somehow we got on the topic of dogs. And for the entire dinner the prince and I gabbed like old friends—about our dogs. Later in the evening, many friends came up to me, all with the same question.

"You two looked so enchanted! What were you talking about?"

Can you imagine their surprise when I smiled and said, "Dogs." Just like that!

Now of all the fans I've interacted with, there is one that stands out above all others—even above the Queen of Soul. So many celebrity fans have found their way to CBS Television City and been guests on our set and that's always been very exciting. We've had professional athletes. Singers. Film stars, politicians. Stars from all different walks of life. Typically when they come they will watch us tape a few scenes and in between takes we come and say hi. Handshakes. Photos. Polite greetings. That's the usual for a VIP.

Well, one day—Muhammad Ali showed up on our very own Studio 43! And unlike any other celebrity before him, the entire production shut down. Let's not forget to mention that time is money and we don't have time to waste on a soap. But when Ali walked onto our set, shooting screeched to a halt. All the guys in the production booth ran from their stations for this once-in-a-lifetime opportunity to shake hands with the great Ali.

The directors, producers, writers, and yes, all of us actors, too, were all giddy at the chance to chat with Ali. He made the biggest impression of any other VIP guest we've ever had, by far. And he was so lovely and humble when he shook my hand.

"Hey Nikki," he said to me in his Ali way. "You're pretty. But I'm prettier."

Ha! I loved it.

And he didn't have a big entourage. I think he had only one person with him. A manager or publicist.

All the VIP male guests can't wait to meet Victor Newman when they visit, and Ali was no exception. I still remember how thrilled he was to shake hands with Eric. And he wasn't at all what you'd think he'd be. He was very quiet, distinguished and respectful and he showed us magic tricks. Yes! He was a magician. I had no idea he knew how to do magic but he was extremely good and took time to entertain us with tricks. On Stage 43 at CBS, with no preparation on his part, I saw Ali literally lift out of his shoes and levitate above ground. I don't know how he did it! It was the best illusion I've ever seen.

He was truly just so gracious and kind. And sure, he was a bit of the Muhammad Ali we'd seen in press interviews, with his witticisms and boastings.

"You know I'm the greatest!" he joked.

Only to us it wasn't a joke. To us he *was* the greatest. Boy, did we enjoy him. That was one of the most exciting days on our set to date.

29

WITH THIS RING I THEE WED

Nikki's been married. *A lot.*

Her first husband was Greg Foster. He was an attorney. In this storyline Nikki erroneously thought she was a client of a reputable modeling agency. But in actuality the agency was a front for a prostitution ring. Of course, Nikki was clueless. The agency sent her out on an "audition." But when she got to the location, there was Walter Addison in a hotel room waiting to have sex with her. She wasn't going to go along with that. One thing led to another and Addison died of a heart attack right in front of her. So there she was with a dead man on the floor and no idea what to do. Turns out that later, her husband defended someone in connection to Addison's death. Greg Foster had no idea that his wife, Nikki, had been present when the man died. It all ended up being a horrific scandal. When Greg finally discovered the truth, he divorced Nikki.

Her next husband was a preppy named Kevin Bancroft. Her marriage to Kevin was arranged by Victor, of all people. Even though Victor loved Nikki, he decided she should marry this nice guy from a good family. He thought it would be the best thing for her. Of course, Nikki did whatever Victor told her to do, so she found herself married to a man she was not in love with.

That storyline began right after I told the show I was pregnant with Alex. This led to the storyline of *Who is the father of Nikki's baby—Victor or Kevin?* Eventually, a DNA test was done, and the father's identity was revealed. It was Victor, of course. Nikki divorced Kevin, and that's what led to Nikki and Victor's first wedding. Baby Victoria (played by the adorable Ashley Millan) was a guest at her parent's first wedding. At two years old, nothing could have been sweeter than seeing her all dolled up at that extravaganza. I still remember it like it was yesterday.

After their wedding, Ashley entered the picture and we had an exciting romantic triangle between Ashley, Nikki, and Victor. Victor ended his marriage to Nikki so he could marry Ashley. On the rebound, Nikki married Jack Abbott.

That was a happy union. For a while, at least. Eventually Nikki became pregnant with Jack's child, a child they both very much wanted. But during a heated discussion with Victor, she fell down the stairs and lost the baby. It was devastating. So devastating that neither she nor Jack could get past it. As a result, they ended up divorcing.

There were many other suitors, boyfriends. Fiancés, too. But the next marriage was to Dr. Joshua Landers. He was Nikki's OB/GYN (I *know* . . . I'd have rather he be *any* other kind of doctor, but what can you do?), and this was the story in which his ex-wife, Veronica, infiltrated Nikki and Dr. Landers' home to work as Nikki's maid. Poor, naive Nikki hired her, not knowing that this woman intended to kill her in an attempt to get her husband, Joshua, back. She did end up shooting Nikki! And at pretty close range, too. Nikki almost died. But of course, she pulled through. Nikki's pulled through after many near-death incidents. She's like a cat with nine lives. Actually, in this analogy, she's had three more husbands than she's had lives!

Nikki's next husband was Victor Newman. And believe it or not they ended up divorcing . . . again.

Next, Nikki married David Chow. God help us. This was the dreadful political storyline where Nikki was running for State Senator. Her husband was her campaign manager. But it eventually came to light that David was an evil guy who was guilty of murdering many people. Apparently he had a plan to murder Nikki, too. He'd been using her for her money the whole time. So as soon as that came out, another marriage was over.

Nikki's like the Energizer Bunny in the marriage department, because she's still going. Her next husband was Deacon Sharpe. Sean Kanan played him *so* beautifully. He's one of my favorite acting partners to work with. Deacon Sharpe was an alcoholic, so when he and Nikki got together it was a lot of drinking, a lot of the time. Deacon actually blackmailed Nikki to go to Vegas and marry him. Nikki agreed but was very unhappy about it. So she drank before, during, and after the wedding ceremony. There was Deacon, so happy and in love, and there was Nikki, a scowling mess through the whole thing. Such a fun storyline! But obviously the marriage didn't last very long.

And would you believe it? Nikki married Jack Abbott. Again! Then they divorced again. And now, bless her heart, Nikki is back with Victor Newman, where she has remained for quite some time.

I know some people might think it's . . . well . . . *ridiculous* that Nikki has been married *so* many times and been in so many different relationships, but hey . . . it's a soap! The complexities of mistakes, especially in love, are one of the commonalities about daytime TV.

As for me—and many people don't know this about me—Edward Scott is my *third* husband. I've been married twice before. Both marriages lasted exactly six months. Both happened before I joined the cast of *Y and R*.

My first marriage was to an actor I had known my whole life, Lindy Davis. We were exactly the same age and had both been child actors. He had a young son who I absolutely adored. I loved that little boy more than I can fully express on these pages. Christian was three years old when Lindy and I got married. But he wasn't even eighteen months old when we started dating, so in many ways, Christian felt like my own son.

I vividly remember our wedding day. It was nothing fancy—just Lindy and me and a few of our closest friends in the Sherman Oaks apartment we shared at the time. We wrote our vows to one another, which wasn't a popular thing to do yet, but it was important to us. I remember that in my vows I pledged my devotion not only to Lindy, but to little Christian, as well. It really was all about family for me. And to be totally honest, the draw to Lindy *was* family. He happened to be the son of my agent, Diane, and her husband, Julian (whom we all fondly called Lefty). They were a wonderful family and had quickly taken me in as their own. They were the first thing in my life that felt like real family to me. It was so wonderful to have Diane at my fortieth *Y and R* anniversary party. Sadly, we lost Lefty to heart surgery in 1987. A devastating blow, as it felt like losing the only father I'd ever known.

I loved Lindy's family. I loved his son. So the decision to leave that marriage after only six months was very difficult. When I did ultimately make the decision to leave, it killed me to know that I would no longer be as close to Christian. He meant everything to me. But the end of our marriage saw an end to the mother-son relationship I had with Christian, and I was left to grieve that unfortunate loss, never able to stop thinking of him.

Now this might sound like something out of the Nikki files, but the officiator at Lindy's and my wedding was Lindy's good friend, Bob Shield. And Bob . . . became my *second* husband.

Chalk it up to dumb youth, as I was seriously dating and living with Bob very soon after leaving Lindy. Yes, it caused controversy. Yes, it ruined their friendship. But when you're young, you live in the moment. You don't think about the long-term effects your rash decisions will have on your life or the lives of others. You simply do what feels good. But in retrospect I was not emotionally ready to jump into a new relationship. And for lack of a more eloquent way to put it, I was just too young to get married. To either one of them.

I take full responsibility for walking away from both of those marriages and leaving some very hurt feelings behind in the process. But again, dumb youth. Besides, Dr. Phil wasn't on the air yet. So where were we supposed to go for advice?! (I certainly hadn't gotten any guidance from my grandmother about dating or marriage.)

It probably didn't help that I remained close with Lindy's family when I began living with Bob. I was still meeting them for biweekly dinners and lunches; the family and I stayed in constant, *regular* contact. I think it seemed to Lindy that they were taking my side rather than his and it caused a lot of hurt feelings.

Of course, I look back now with older eyes and see my attraction was to Lindy's family. I was able to let him go but not them. They were the real loves of my life. Because you see, at this young age, I'd only known neglect and abuse. Lindy's family showed me love. I craved that.

My relationship with Bob was an easy one. He truly adored me and made that very clear. If I hadn't been so young and impetuous, we may have lasted a lifetime, because Bob truly was a man with a heart of gold. I hope that he went on to marry a wonderful woman, create a beautiful family, and has led a happy life. I really do. I harbor no ill will for either one of them. But with Bob there was a maturity that I hadn't experienced before. He took care of me. I never questioned his love. I was just ready to move on. But I'll admit that leaving that relationship was very hard. And I regret hurting Bob the way I did. I regret hurting both of them. But ultimately I have always been the type who listens to my inner soul. Neither relationship felt . . . right. I had to move on.

It was, of course, different when I met Edward. He felt like a grown-up and I did, too. Sometimes life is about timing, and Edward and I met at a time in our lives where the stars were aligned for us. That's the best way to describe it!

I have a little side story I'm eager to tell you: In 1980, just a year into my time at *Y and R*, I met with the psychic Beverly Eilbacher just for fun. She was actually the mother of an actress that I had grown up with in the business, Cindy Eilbacher, who would eventually play April Stevens on our show (under the name Cynthia Jordan). As we sat in her Beverly Hills kitchen, Beverly read my tarot cards and tea leaves, the latter of which had never been read for me before. After careful consideration she closed her eyes and started to tell me what she *saw*.

"Melody, I've known you since you were four years old and I've always adored you. I can see the engagement ring on your finger and I know how excited you are to be getting married." (This was right before my marriage to Bob.) "But I have to tell you that this marriage is *not* the one. It won't last. Your *next* marriage will stand the test of time and you will be very happy."

This news didn't sit well with me. I looked down lovingly at my engagement ring.

Beverly continued, her eyes still closed.

"You already know this man I am speaking of. He works in your business, in a position of authority, on the other side of the camera. He has one daughter."

I couldn't imagine who on earth she could be talking about. The only man I knew that fit that description was my publicist, Bob Olive. And as much fun as we had working together, I couldn't believe that he and I would ever get married!

Time passed. Beverly's prediction was forgotten.

Years later, after Edward and I had married in 1985, I ran into

Beverly by chance. Upon seeing her face, everything she had said to me the last time I saw her came rushing back to me.

"Oh, Beverly! Can you believe that every single thing you told me that day in your kitchen came *true?!*"

She looked at me blankly and said, "What did I tell you?"

I tried to refresh her memory. But she didn't respond as I hoped she would.

"Melody, I'm so glad that you and Ed are happy. But when I do a reading I go into a trance and I never remember any of it."

Yes, the other side does have its mysterious ways!

Edward and I actually renewed our wedding vows in 2005. A TV special was produced around it and the whole event was aired on CBS as a primetime special. We both thought that it was somewhat silly because we're still together and in love and . . . this marriage needs to be reinstated? Obviously, it was not our idea. CBS contacted us out of the blue to do this, in Las Vegas, and they kept expanding the details of the deal. We resisted at first. Renewing vows in Vegas didn't sound like something we would ever do. CBS was determined, though: increasing the money, sweetening the accommodations, and the best part—we could invite as many of our friends as we wanted from all over the country, and they'd pay for everything. Eventually we thought, "Well, okay, it sounds like it could be really fun." So we were wooed into it.

The network gave me a beautiful, original Reem Acra gown to wear for the ceremony, and it still hangs in my closet today. One of the sponsors was a jeweler, and they gave me a $35,000 diamond ring. There were a lot of perks involved, and I didn't even know about the ring until we got there. I ended up losing that ring a few months later. Edward and I were flying to Rome for Christmas, and I left the ring on the sink in the ladies room of Alitalia's VIP lounge at LAX. I had taken it off to wash my hands, promptly forgotten about it, went back to my seat in the lounge, and realized it was missing maybe three or four minutes later. I ran back to the bath-room, but it was gone. I told the people in the lounge, but I never heard anything more about it. So that was quite a find for someone.

Back to Las Vegas . . . The whole thing turned out to be lovely. We had a huge, beautiful suite, they flew in all of our friends from ev-erywhere, and we had a series of blow-out parties. It *was* fun and great to have all of our friends right there with us. But the essence of why we were there, to renew our vows, we weren't really all that into. But the network was.

Lost ring aside, renewing the vows turned out to be a wonderful experience. Despite our reluctance, it was very special to declare, once again, that we wanted to spend the rest of our lives with one another.

Together forever. That seems to be our deal.

30

PETER BERGMAN

Since Nikki's been married to Jack a few times, I have to tell a fun story about Peter Bergman. Terry Lester, our original Jack Abbott, chose to leave the show for personal reasons. Jack was a huge character for *Y and R* and it was devastating to lose Terry. I knew that the show was looking for a new Jack. I thought, hmmm. What large shoes to fill. Good luck with that . . .

One weekend Edward and I were in Toronto, having dinner with a dear friend of ours, Lilana Novakovich. She brought a copy of that week's *Soap Opera Digest* and had it sitting on the table. I picked it up and stumbled upon a story. *All My Children* had fired Peter Bergman? *What*? I had watched Peter on *All My Children* for years and thought he was such a wonderful actor. Fired? I couldn't believe it. At that moment I knew we had found our new Jack Abbott.

When we got back to L.A., I presented the idea to production.

"I know who our new Jack Abbott is," I declared. "You simply have to meet with Peter Bergman."

Now, I'd never met Peter, but after watching him for years on *All My Children* it *felt* like I knew him. His character on *All My Children*, Cliff, was quite honestly nothing like Jack. Cliff Warner was nice and upstanding and, well, Jack was not. But I knew there was something in him. Just by watching him work, I was convinced he'd be a perfect Jack.

Apparently everyone agreed that it would be crazy not to have him at least audition. He seemed to fit everything the show was looking for in a replacement. So they flew him to Los Angeles for a talent test. Meanwhile his wife, Mariellen, was in New York City expecting their second child at literally any moment. Along with his sudden firing, what a whirlwind he must have been experiencing. But his talent test was phenomenal. And he got the part. And, of course, he's still on the show to this day.

Whenever he's doing interviews he very generously says, "I'm only here because of Melody Thomas Scott."

That's typical Peter. He's a gracious, well-liked professional, and has won several Emmys as Jack.

He never knew why *AMC* let him go. They never explained it to him. But it was their loss. He got the part of Jack, his wife had the baby, and the next week they moved cross-country to Los Angeles. It was one of those synchronistic, meant-to-be things that happen in life sometimes. I was pleased to play a part in it.

Peter could play a nice guy on *AMC* and a bad guy on *Y and R* with equal success. And I always assume the whole world must know this story, but a lot of the fans don't seem to.

Now they do.

31

THE GAMES PEOPLE PLAY

A lot of our cast members have guested on other shows, playing ourselves. I did episodes of *The Nanny*, *The King of Queens*, and *Diagnosis: Murder*. They were all great fun. I'm a *huge* Dick Van Dyke fan from his sixties sitcom, *The Dick Van Dyke Show*. Just to meet him and work with him was incredible. Alex was also a huge fan because of *Mary Poppins*, so she wanted to meet him, too. I got her up at 4 a.m. the morning of the shoot, practically dragging her out of bed. She made it to the car grasping her well-worn VHS copy of *Mary Poppins* and we were excitedly on our way. Meeting him was such a thrill for her. And as you would expect, he was the absolute sweetest. He hugged her, signed her video, and even chatted with her for a bit.

Doing guest shots on other shows is always a nice change of pace. But I must admit, what I love even more are game shows. In general, I would say there was never a game show I did that I didn't love. I'm simply in my element being a contestant on a game show. To me, it's the most fun in the world. And I really mean that—they were all such a joy for me. A lot of actors are advised by their agents not to do them because the agent believes it lessens their clients' star power. But that was never said directly to me, and I wouldn't have cared anyway. It was the best time of my life.

One of my favorite things about being on a television show like *Y and R* was being invited to do game shows. I grew up watching them, and when I first hired Bob Olive, my publicist, I told him that that was my golden wish. He didn't think booking me would be too difficult. Then I told him that *The $10,000 Pyramid* was my absolute dream. He explained that *that* booking would be more difficult, as the producers, which included Dick Clark, cared equally about the guest celebrity's ability to play the game well, along with what their show biz pedigree was.

Being on *Pyramid*, which kept increasing its grand prize and title (to *$25,000* and then *$100,000*), was my ultimate desire. Bob arranged for me to do a "test game" where I met the booking agent from the show and played the game casually in an office setting. I thought I had played the game well, but we never heard anything back from them. Or so Bob told me! He was so delightfully sneaky—he *had* heard back from them already but he hadn't told me, wanting to save my surprise . . . they wanted to book me on *Pyramid*, my life-long fantasy! He had actually booked me several weeks in advance without telling me. About a week before the tapings he casually asked me, "Hey, what are you doing on Saturday?"

"Nothing."

"Want to be on *Pyramid* with Dick Clark?"

I was screaming! I was jumping up and down! I was over the moon. And it was great. Dick Clark was a doll, a wonderful host, and as a producer, he ran a tight ship. We were all on time or else.

When shooting a game show, you'd shoot five, maybe ten episodes on the same day, back-to-back. We had about five minutes between shows to change outfits. We brought five changes of clothes so that it would look like every show was shot on a different day. The viewers at home probably never knew that we were shooting them all in one day. But in reality, of course, that's how game shows are done.

I do believe *Pyramid* was *the* best game show, but I also believe there was something in my brain that really clicked into the format of that game more than any other I've done. I don't mean to boast, but when all was said and done, I held the record for winning our contestants the most combined money. My brain isn't necessarily wired for normal life, but it sure was wired for that show!

I'd still play it today if I could, though the last time I played *Pyramid* I discovered they had changed the methodology of the game and I was no longer interested.

There was also *Family Feud*. I was booked to do *Family Feud* in the beginning with Richard Dawson hosting, and then later with the late Ray Combs, a wonderful man and friend who I adored.

When my daughter Alex was around two, some friends of mine and I were in Palm Springs for the weekend. Apparently I got way too much sun—we had been out by the pool, swimming and playing. My girlfriend Gwen had friends who lived locally and we were invited to their home for dinner that night. At their dinner table, I started to feel unwell and excused myself to use the bathroom. I didn't get very far. I passed out on the living room carpet en route to the bathroom. They called 911.

Severe heat stroke was my official diagnosis. When you have that, you throw up a lot, and when I came to, I was doing just that. Throwing up, a lot. Someone at the table had brought me a plastic bowl to throw up into. At the same time I was vomiting, an episode of *Family Feud* that featured me came on their television. So there I am, sick on their living room floor, but also on their TV competing on *Family Feud*. And our hostess, who was a huge *Y and R* fan cries out, "Oh, no, no, no, not a plastic bowl for Nikki!"

And she runs and gets a *silver* bowl. Truth! She took the plastic bowl from my hands and presented me with a beautiful, sterling silver bowl. To vomit into. This is how fans are—only the best bowl in the house would do for Nikki Newman. I'll never forget that moment: my virtual self happily playing *Family Feud* while my real self was splayed out on the carpet of a stranger's home, a sterling silver bowl of vomit at my side.

One week, *Family Feud* was doing a week's worth of shows with cast members from *Y and R* on one side and *The Price Is Right* on the other. Having worked at CBS's TV City as long as I have, I know how Bob Barker was—he wasn't what you saw on TV. In real life, I'm afraid to say, he was nothing like what you'd imagine.

In any event, we're all playing for charity. Each player on the *Y and R* team had selected their favorite charity to play for, which is the standard protocol for celebrity teams. I was playing for the Save the Earth Foundation. I noticed that *The Price Is Right* team was playing for the same charity every day rather than individual charities for their individual team players. I found out later that the girls on *The Price Is Right* (at the time they were called "Barker's Beauties") were not allowed to play for their own charities. Bob forced them to play each of the five days for *his* charity.

So we're playing the game. Not far into the first show, I'm thinking, *what's going on?* I'm sure you've seen *Family Feud*—you have a certain amount of time to guess the answer, and if you answer incorrectly, the other team gets a chance to steal. Well, that's how it went when our team was answering. But not Bob's team. When they got something wrong, there was no buzzer. There was a long pause, and then the producer (in the audience) would call out, "Ohhh, you're close, try again."

Try again?!—What? No! There's no try again. What do you mean, try again? It was totally unfair. And this continued! They were given as many chances as it took for them to come up with the right answer. We were never given this courtesy. And it wouldn't have been fair if we had. Of course they were going to edit out these second and third chances. The viewers at home would never see this nonsense. I'm quite competitive, but I believe in total fairness. I was fuming mad—I had never experienced this kind of thing when shooting a game show, and I had played them all! You can be sure Dick Clark would never have allowed this.

Of course, Barker's team won that first day, Monday. Everyone on my team had noticed what was going on as well, but they were afraid to say anything. But then there's me and my mouth. I made my way down to the executive producer seated in the audience and accused him of cheating. He had not one word to say to me. His mouth literally dropped open in silence. And, wouldn't you know, on Tuesday's show, *my* charity won (the only show that any of the *Y and R* charities *did* win that entire week). Which, I think, was a little crooked as well. I'm confident that they let my charity win because of my accusation. The rest of the week, the pendulum swung back to Barker's team. More *blatant* cheating.

When we finally finished taping all five episodes, I went back to the EP and said, "Whoever decided to allow my charity to win, uh, thanks for that. However," I paused in an effort to contain my growing rage, "you are unbelievable cheaters, and a disgrace to the game show industry."

Apparently, he was still rendered speechless from my earlier tirade. All he gave me was that same befuddled look, complete with a gaping mouth. No words. Then again, what could he have said? I'm sure he thought, what gall this lady has! We'll make sure to never book *her* again. But then, I had already made the decision to never play *their* show again.

32

KRISTOFF

The tragic death of Kristoff St. John in 2019 was a crushing blow to our *Y and R* family. Many of us are still grieving. Perhaps the grieving will never end. I think with grief you can reach a point of emotional overload, and you have to find a way to protect your emotions so you can move on with life. And that, too, is painful. On top of the grief, you feel this crushing, all-consuming guilt. Even as I type these words I find my eyes welling with tears and my heart breaking all over again.

If the initial shock wasn't enough, communing with the *Y and R* family just intensified our emotions. We were all so broken. A couple of weeks later, we shot an episode (not an official *Y and R* episode) that was a compilation of our individual tributes to Kristoff; a few days later, we shot Neil's funeral and funeral reception. And a few weeks later, we all attended his real-life funeral. This just kept forcing our pain to the surface.

I was thinking about Kristoff all the time. He had such a light in and around him, such a vibrant and loving energy. It's difficult to put into words. You just wanted to be around him. You wanted to soak up his aura because it was so brilliant. You know those kinds of people who just light up a room, who make your darkest days brighter? Kristoff was that. He had such wisdom and such a unique perspective on the complexities of life. Whenever there was a *Y and R* gathering, I'd greet others and then immediately ask, "Where's Kristoff?"

I always wanted to be where Kristoff was. If you were around him, *that* was where the most fun was going to happen. What an enthusiasm for life he had. What a positive perspective he maintained. He enjoyed having deep and meaningful discussions, too. We could discuss the meaning of life, aliens, metaphysics. You name it. He'd be game for an intense chat on more or less any subject. Kristoff St. John was my friend. We understood each other. He was a very special human being, and I loved working with him. I loved *him*.

Our characters shared a connection in that both Nikki and Neil were alcoholics. We had some beautiful, touching scenes together encompassing that. Everyone loved working with Kristoff. He was a delightful human being and a phenomenal actor. He was always in the moment, in the scene. You'd throw something off-script at him and he'd be right on it and ready for wordplay. With Kristoff there were never any on-screen thoughts of, *do you think we'll get there? Will we get to that emotion? Is this scene working?* No, with Kristoff it *always* worked. With the two of us in a scene, everything else would disappear. No cameras, no crew, it was just Kristoff and me. There are certain parts of his character and his abilities that I don't have words for. It was all very magical. He was a magical guy.

I don't think anyone knew that he had heart problems. I don't even know if *he* knew, as it was never a topic of discussion between us. But from the time his son died so tragically back in 2014, we were all concerned for Kristoff. As parents, we can't imagine the reality of that, of losing a child. And he had great difficulty dealing with such a heartbreaking loss, as anyone would. He showed a lot of fragility during that time. I mean, he was our brother, and we loved him, so we would keep tabs on him. Sort of a universal . . .

How's Kristoff?

Where is he?

What is he doing this weekend?

Have we checked in with Kristoff?

During that initial period of grief, after he lost his son, there were times when we *couldn't* reach him. We would all be so afraid, thinking he was missing, and it would turn out . . .

"Oh, he's at so-and-so's house. He's fine!"

But there were a lot of calls to go to his home and make sure he was OK. We stayed close to him during that time. As far as his death—it is a tragedy that I don't think I'll ever get over. His funeral service was held in a church that holds hundreds of people. There were so many mourners. So many got up and spoke beautiful words about him. Even his father, who is also an actor and also a wonderful human being. It was heart-wrenching. I remember thinking that if I were in his father's shoes, I wouldn't have been able to get up and do that so eloquently. But that's just how amazing Kristoff was. I know his father's grief was so intense, but he didn't want to give up his opportunity to talk about his only child. To share the wonder of this extraordinary human who had touched all of our lives.

I know he's watching over me as I type these words. Reading over my shoulder. And yes, we were a family, with the ups and downs that come with being a family. But we loved him. We loved him so much.

I must share that when we did the *Y and R* tribute episode, our wardrobe department asked if I wanted them to select an outfit for me or instead bring something of my own. I offered to bring my own wardrobe since it wasn't a traditional episode. I just grabbed a dress out of my closet, with no forethought. After the episode, I placed it back into my closet with a tag labeling the date I wore it on air. Just for my records.

Fast forward to Kristoff's real-life funeral. Again, I grabbed a suit from my closet with no thought as to what I was putting on. I sat next to Eric and Doug Davidson at the church. At one point I took my jacket off and laid it across my lap. I looked down at the label, and it said *St. John*.

I turned to Doug and Eric and I said, "Look! Look at this label."

They thought I had worn it intentionally.

A month or two later, I was cleaning out my closet and came across the outfit I wore on the tribute episode. I studied it for a moment, realizing it, too, was St. John! I have hundreds of dresses in my wardrobe, but very few items from that designer. What were the odds? I decided it was the power of Kristoff. It was a sign.

He was letting me know that he was still with me.

33

GOING OFF ON A TANGENT

Since we're on the subject of Kristoff, can I tell you that he enjoyed going off on a tangent with me?

I've always been known as an actress who can cry at the drop of the hat, which serves me well on a soap opera. The writers have used my ability to produce instantaneous tears to their advantage. I honestly think crying is easier to do in a scene than laughing. Tears have always been so easily accessible to me. After so many years of being called upon to cry, I started to look for other challenges. Like . . . hmm. Crying is easy. But crying a single tear? On the downstage cheek? Can I do *that*?! After much sorting out of the mechanics in my head, I finally could.

After doing it for so long, people have started to ask me *how* I do it. So I've decided to tell all in this book. Here's the answer. Finally. The secret to my single tear.

I have no idea!

I'm in the moment, I'm being Nikki, I'm thinking about why Nikki is crying and suddenly *I'm* crying. I'm sorry to disappoint, but there's no big secret. I'd say it's just acting, but, more importantly, it's BELIEVING.

Another very Mel thing to do is to go off-script. To improvise. Now don't get me wrong. I'm not a writer. Our writers do their job and they do it *beautifully*. I'm simply taking *their* words and going off on a tangent, if you will. When an actor you're working with "goes off on a tangent," you have to be *listening*. To be able to play that ping-pong word game, to have a response for off-scripted moments, you have to be paying attention. I'm always up for that challenge. Eric is, as well, and is the master! So was Kristoff. Kristoff loved that sort of "living on the edge" feeling in a scene.

We both had an affinity for that live television zone that you have to be in when going with the flow like that. You have to be sharp to have an immediate comeback. Some actors can't do it. They get thrown off track if the words aren't exactly as they appear on the page. I call them "by the book" actors. No judgment. Any type of in-the-moment acting, whether on script or off, is worthy of praise. But when you discover an actor who likes to play, it's just so much fun. It brings some punch to the scenes and adds a fresh layer of reality that I think really draws the viewers in.

A lot of people comment on the "Niktor" chemistry. I think *this* is at the heart of us. Eric and I are so used to one another that we often "go off on a tangent." It keeps our scenes so alive and real. Sometimes we're crying, sometimes we're yelling, but it's 100% organic. During those moments our chemistry is on fire. It might take the producers by surprise, but they'll still air it because it's so authentically Nikki and Victor.

Think of it like a "scripted improvisation." The reason it works so well with us is because we have built a foundation of trust. We know we can trust each other to respond properly, according to the story, no matter what words we say. It's never planned. Sure, the scripted lines are in our head and they're what ultimately guide us. And it's nice that they don't stop tape but instead recognize that we're amping up the emotional impact of the scene. Plus, it's nice to feel like a part of the creative team. We have the freedom as actors to contribute to the magic that is attributed to our characters. What more could an actor ask for?

And I have to hand it to Peter Bergman. He's phenomenal and also loves to "go off on a tangent," but in an entirely different way. With Peter, he can find emotions that you didn't know existed within the scene. I had the pleasure of experiencing this fairly recently with him. I couldn't imagine the emotion that the director wanted could be found in that scene. I just didn't see it. I remember saying, "Hey, don't hold your breath. No tears will be shed here."

But Peter gave me such underlying emotion, such unexpected layers. It elevated my response and the scene turned out to be terrific. I was crying so intensely that I could barely say my lines.

The director came out right after that, and said, "And you were worried?!"

I admitted, "I have only Peter to thank."

Some actors do that: they take your emotions to another level and allow you to go with them on that ride. And what a glorious ride that can be! I am blessed that so many of our *Y and R* actors know how to do that.

34

PRESCRIPTION FOR MADNESS

I had been sick with a sinus infection for several days, suffering with a terrible, guttural cough that I couldn't shake. I'd missed some work which, in Hollywood, is unacceptable. You're half dead? You can *perhaps* miss an episode or two. Otherwise, get your ass out of bed and to the studio. This time, I *was* half dead. There was no way I was making it to CBS.

But missing work on a soap greatly alters *everyone's* schedule since we shoot multiple episodes in a week. I hated to be home sick.

"You have to see a doctor," everyone insisted. My husband, my coworkers, my friends.

"I'd love to," I'd said. "Who should I go to?"

"Don't you have a doctor?"

"No, do you?"

"Well, no."

I was having this same conversation, over and over, and it was enough to drive me mad. But nobody seems to have doctors that they can recommend anymore! Ones that they *would* recommend, any- way. Finally, my husband suggested a doctor he'd heard good things about, Dr. Black. *OK, fine. I'll go see Dr. Black.* Little did I know that I was headed into one of the most harrowing experiences of my life.

Nathan, my assistant, drove me to the doctor's office. Edward left work early to meet us there. They had to sneak me in through the back of the medical building so I could have privacy. It's one thing to be very ill, and another thing entirely to have your unknown illness splashed across tabloids.

They did a chest X-ray, a lung capacity test, and heart and lung assessments. Certain illnesses were ruled out. But I was croupy. I wheezed terribly every time I exhaled and sounded horrible.

Dr. Black didn't seem overly concerned. I told him I was prone to sinus infections but that I had never had one as bad as this one before. His reaction was rather nonchalant. In fact, I got the distinct feeling he just wanted me in and out as soon as possible. When he'd completed his exam, he sent me home with three prescriptions:

Cough syrup with codeine. I'd had this many times over the years.

Augmentin. This was an antibiotic I'd never had before. Or even heard of.

And finally, Cadista. A steroid. Never had this one before, either.

Nathan took me home to rest while he filled the prescriptions at the pharmacy. True, I hadn't been crazy about the doctor, but I was relieved that I might be on the road to recovery soon.

However, the steroid made me anxious and irritable. I called Dr. Black.

"This medication is making me feel very strange," I explained. "Are you sure it's okay?"

"Continue taking all three medications," he said.

Well, okay, I thought. *Doctor knows best.* I had no real reason to distrust him, and by this point I was desperate. I listened. I continued with the medications.

By that evening I was hallucinating.

Lying in bed in my room, I was convinced I'd been somehow magically transported to Texas, or maybe Mexico. I knew it was one of the two.

The paranoia set in next. Not only was I in Texas (or maybe Mexico), I was confident "they" were coming to get me. I didn't know who "they" were or *why* they were coming, but I knew I was in grave danger.

I got out of bed repeatedly. I would tiptoe to the balcony, listen at the screen door. Waiting. For what? Why, a pack of men who I knew were down below ready to scurry up the trellis, break in, and kidnap me, of course.

In addition, my head was spinning with dizziness. I was disoriented. I was confused and afraid. I could barely move except for the moments when I'd step carefully to peek out through the balcony, waiting for "them."

Here's where things got even scarier.

There *was* no balcony in my bedroom. No screen door either. None of it was real, not even the room I was trying to sleep in. My whole sense of who I was and where I was became a fantasy. But I remember it clearly. Vividly in fact. I can close my eyes and picture myself in that room, watching repeats of *Family Feud* and *Ocean's 11*. Only there was no TV. The television and the programs were a part of the hallucination. But that didn't stop me from watching them. With perfect clarity I sat and watched a TV that didn't exist. In a room I was completely imagining. In Mexico.

While hallucinating, you aren't actually aware that you *are* hallucinating. It's very real to you. You truly believe these things are happening to and around you. But by the time you figure it out, it is a *terrifying* realization. Reliving it now sends chills up my spine.

Some might call what I was experiencing some sort of psychotic meltdown. I kept wondering if I was dying. Then I'd decide, no. I'm not dying. But maybe I'm crazy? I'd shrug that off. No, no. I'm not crazy. People really are trying to get me. But why?! I couldn't for the life of me understand why I was being pursued by the bad guys or what I was doing in Mexico.

What was happening is that I was reacting to the medication I'd been given. It would take me some time before I came to the conclusion that I'd been floxed—fluoroquinolone toxicity syndrome. The devastating effects of a class of antibiotics that alone can cause nervous system disturbances. Mixed with other drugs, it led to my waking nightmare.

After a difficult night in which I got little sleep, I got out of bed the next morning and knew immediately that I was in no condition to even leave my room. I was slipping deeper and deeper into my hallucinations. I was fatigued, and my cough was worse than ever. Memories and thoughts were tough to hold onto. I stayed in bed. I watched more TV. Mind you, there was no TV.

By that evening, my family was keyed in to me being "out of my mind," if you will. To say they were concerned would be an understatement. But what did they do? They told me to keep taking my medicine. That would be the key to my healing. Doctor knows best, right?

"You'll feel better, Mom, just keep taking your medicine," Alex said.

"Take your medicine, doll," Edward said.

This is what they advised. Hell, if I'd have been in my right mind, I would have advised that, too. How could we have known? How could anyone know? Medicine is meant to treat your ailments, not cause them.

Another day passed and I was not getting any better. I was getting worse. Dizziness, nausea, hallucinations. Everything was closing in, getting smaller, scarier. I remember being awake for most of the night, hallucinating about where we were and how we were going to get out. I was in my own home of fifteen years, but my mind was somewhere else. I was lost.

"I'm in danger," I remember whispering to myself, my eyes darting back and forth. "There are people outside of this room, and they're trying to get me."

In the morning I begged Edward to lead us to safety. "We've got to get out of here!" I cried.

Wise, wise Edward. Clearly he was taken aback, but he played along.

"Absolutely, doll. I will get us to safety. Okay?"

"Oh, thank you," I said. I remember feeling at ease knowing that he was on it and that he would protect me from "them."

"But do you know how to get out?" I asked seriously.

He assured me that he did. God bless him. How he must've felt in those moments. Thankfully he gathered the family and let them know that something very serious was happening with me. And suddenly there they all were, rallying around me. I was barely lucid enough to connect, but I knew that they were there.

I couldn't eat. I was literally starting to lose my taste buds. What they did force on me I threw up. The vomiting was so violent and intense that I couldn't find moments to breathe. Projectile. I became certain that death was imminent.

My husband called the doctor, because clearly the medicine wasn't working. They discussed the possibility that I was suffering from a severe reaction to the medication, particularly the steroids, and decided that I should stop taking them immediately. Good call.

I wish I could say that my troubles ended once I stopped the medication. They did not. I hid under blankets on the sofa. I was so cold. I remember the feeling that my skin was freezing. The hallucinations continued. Of course I wasn't consciously aware of this. I thought the visions were real. I *would* try to engage in conversations that were happening around me, though I'm sure my family members saw it as senseless babbling.

And then the nausea kicked up a notch.

I felt so sick that I couldn't catch my breath. Unable to breathe properly, panic set in. My family rushed me to the emergency room. When we arrived, I couldn't get out of the car or walk on my own.

Someone brought out a wheelchair, which at least got me through the hospital doors. My condition must've seemed dire because the staff took me in right away.

Questions were thrown at me:

"Do you know where you are?"

"What's today's date?"

"Who's the president?"

I was in the hospital. That I knew. Who is the president? I smiled up at the doctor, of course I knew that! But as soon as I tried to answer, my mind went blank. Who *was* the president? It beat the hell outta me. I'm not even sure I knew my own name.

More doctors came into the room. More questions were asked. I was poked and prodded and poked some more. Finally Edward, who'd had enough, asked, "What's the verdict? Can she go home now?"

"Home?" The doctor looked at him straight-on. "Mr. Scott," he stressed, "Your wife doesn't even know who she is."

Cedars—and probably every major hospital—has certain criteria a patient must meet before they are admitted. Some of my indications looked suspicious for meningitis, so that had to be ruled out. A spinal tap was first up on my agenda. Edward is not as good with pain as I am, and he was panicking when he found out a spinal tap had been ordered for me. I wasn't concerned—I didn't have the energy to be concerned. I only had a vague awareness of what was happening to me.

If I had been lucid, the spinal tap probably would've been excruciating—I'm sure there's nothing pleasant about a needle in your spine, extracting fluid. But I felt nothing. Thankfully the tests for meningitis came back negative. They did discover that I had no electrolytes left in my body, though. Hypokalemia is the medical term. Totally dehydrated. Apparently my level was a record low. How was I even alive? I was given an IV for fluids.

My entire day was filled with tests. The maddening thing was that once I was officially their patient, I was at their mercy. All I wanted to do was go home so I could die in peace since I just knew that I was dying. And I couldn't have imagined a worse way to go, stuck in a freezing cold hospital away from the comforts of home. I wanted to be back in my bed. Hell, being back in Mexico staring out onto the imaginary balcony through its screen door was better than this. But instead I was a new prisoner with a team of doctors and nurses as my wardens.

I remember them telling me they were going to take me to some other room for further testing. *More* tests?

Soon, all of my family arrived. I know my children. And as confused as I was, I could see the fear in their eyes. I knew. They knew. My situation was dire.

The day slowly dragged on. The tests continued. They were quite thorough. I was tested for brain disorders, stroke, and seizures; I was given MRIs, CT scans, and anything else they could think of. No expense was spared; no test was left undone. But everything came back normal. Nevertheless, I continued vomiting. I was still having a hard time breathing. I was still hallucinating. I was convinced that I was dying and there was nothing anybody could do to stop it.

Instead of a typical private room, it was decided that a private room on an isolation *floor* was best. I was too out of it to even be aware of it. I just wanted to go home. What passed next was the longest, most uncomfortable night of my life. Sleep was impossible. Doctors and nurses were coming in constantly, asking if my heart rate was "always this low." I've never had heart problems, and I still don't. Perhaps I could've died that night. My heart almost seemed as if it was slowing to a stop.

Eventually, they brought me food. Though I was starving, every morsel was inedible. Actually, that's not exactly true . . . having lost my taste buds, everything tasted like *nothing*. At that point it becomes all about texture, and all textures brought on more nausea. Nothing stayed down. Instead of sleeping, I spent that first night in the hospital moaning and writhing around in pain—or trying to, with IV's in both of my arms connecting me to machines on either side of me. I remember the bed was equipped with some kind of alarm that would yell out, "Stay in bed! Do not stand up!"

I laid in pain, in agony, waiting for a nurse to assist me. Edward spent the night in my room on a cot. I can't fault him for sleeping, but it was a strange sort of distance to have someone there sleeping peacefully as I pondered life and death. Still hallucinating, I watched as that room changed shape and dynamics all night long.

The tests continued into the next day. I could not make sense of the nurse "call" buttons or other controls connected to the bed— they had no meaning to me. I needed Edward to push the buttons. Even though he showed me how to do it over and over again, I couldn't remember any of it.

Throughout the whole ordeal, I never saw Dr. Black even once. And he was on the hospital's staff! He knew that I was reacting badly to the medicine he'd prescribed. Edward had kept him up to speed. But apparently having one of his new patients admitted to the hospital was of no concern to him.

It got to the point where, any time a doctor came into the room, no matter who they were, I grabbed their arm and begged them to release me. I'm sure that sounds dramatic, but I was a desperate woman. They weren't actually helping me, anyway. I was the same. There were no improvements and no answers. I really was a prisoner.

There were so many tests, so many vials of blood extracted. So many questions unanswered. No doctor had any idea what was wrong with me. They finally decided there was nothing they could actually do to help me. My heart rate had stabilized and so they decided to grant my request for release. But as they wheeled me toward the exit of the hospital, I threw up again. All over the lobby carpet. Just a little parting gift from me . . .

I was grateful to be home, but I obviously wasn't ready to resume any sort of normal life. Jill Farren Phelps, the executive producer of *Y and R* at the time, called to check on me. Edward answered the phone. I remember him holding out the phone to me. I knew what it was. A phone. I remember thinking, *this is a phone.* But that thought was immediately followed by, *what on Earth do I do with it?* Technology made no sense to me: phones, computers, remote controls—any sort of gadget with buttons and numbers . . . forget about it. It was like learning to walk all over again.

I wasn't any better and I continued to hallucinate. It was clear that I couldn't return to work. In fact, I was getting more and more concerned that I'd never be able to work again. What was to become of me?

Days went by. Eventually, a script was delivered by production. Edward said it was on the kitchen counter. But when I stepped in there, I was transported back to the kitchen of another house we'd lived in twenty years earlier. I looked around the room. Had I traveled through time? *No, no.* I shook it off. You're not well. Have a seat. Read your script. You'll get through this. That was the lucid part of me. Because rational me said: *You really have no idea what you're doing. Acting? Reading?! Good luck.*

It was only two pages of dialogue with my darling Doug Davidson. One scene. That's it. I read it. Or, rather, attempted to. I couldn't wrap my head around the words that were on the page. I distinctly remember becoming overwhelmed with emotion. I thought my career might be over. I might never work again. I had to seek out help. *Real* help.

Because the medical community offered nothing to help me, we decided we'd have to turn to alternative medicine. Edward got on the phone, collecting information from friends, and found that two of them had suffered from this very same thing. These very same steroids. The very same antibiotic. Perhaps this "rare" reaction wasn't so rare after all. The Bell family told us about an exceptional acupuncturist located in Santa Monica. I'd had good results in the past with acupuncture, so I was eager to meet with Dr. Hoffman as soon as possible.

We made the appointment. I, of course, was unable to drive, so Edward drove me to the office while I laid in the backseat. My husband practically had to drag me from the car to the office as I could hardly stand on my own. I entered the doctor's office, hanging onto Edward, moaning and groaning, and collapsed onto a sofa. As Dr. Hoffman approached, I was crying.

"Are you the doctor?" I sobbed.

"Yes, I am." His voice was calming.

"Please, help me."

"I will."

There was something in his voice. I felt assured. I felt hope.

With Edward and Alex there to relay most of my story, Dr. Hoffman thoroughly surmised the situation. Against one wall, he had a large piece of furniture with dozens of tiny drawers. With each symptom explained, Dr. Hoffman went to a new drawer for herbs, which he put inside tiny, clear capsules. Every day, I had to take them. And every day I started to get a little bit better. The almost daily acupuncture treatments were helping, too. There were only slight improvements at first, but I could feel the difference. I was so grateful.

We added massage therapy. Ninety minutes a day. Again, there was a slight improvement in my general condition. Massage. Acupuncture. Herbs. Now Alex got online and found a yoga instructor, and I started seeing her multiple times a week as well. Time was passing. I was *healing*.

I have also, on the advice of Dr. Hoffman, switched my diet to dairy-free, all organic foods, including lots of kale and other super-foods. The change in my energy has been remarkable.

I'm excited to tell you that for my second appointment with Dr. Hoffman, I walked in on my own. It was sort of a slow, zombie-like dragging motion, but I did it on my own.

And that is how I recovered. *This* is how I found my way to healing.

Right before I went back to work, I posted a long update on my Facebook page. I wanted my fans to know why I had been absent and what I'd been dealing with. And, most importantly, I wanted others to know the risks of certain medications—risks that the medical community didn't warn me about. Risks they kept denying.

Immediately, comments started pouring in:

"Oh, you're a floxie!"

"I'm a floxie too!"

"I didn't know I was a floxie until it was too late."

The same word, over and over again: floxie.

I responded to comments and conversed with fans, then did a little research on my own. Finally, finally, I was able to piece together what had happened to me.

The term floxie comes from a class of drug, fluoroquinolones. They're used to treat a whole slew of things: urinary tract infections, skin infections, respiratory infections, you name it. Sinus infections, too. These potentially deadly drugs are prescribed to *millions*. Year after year. Unfortunately, some of those people negatively affected by these drugs never recover. The rest of their lives are spent suffering. Or, worst case scenario, their lives come to an end. But now that so many cases have been revealed, it looks like the medical community might finally be realizing the error of their ways and putting warnings in place for unsuspecting patients.

I did finally, at last, stop hallucinating. I began eating again. I returned to work full-time after the New Year. My neurological breakdown had finally reversed. But it was a long and difficult recovery.

During my illness, I missed my *Y and R* family. I missed my *life*. I couldn't have pulled through without Edward or Dr. Hoffman, or the love and support of my children and so many others. But this should not have to happen to anyone else ever again. If the medical and pharmaceutical communities won't do their jobs and put warnings in place, then I hope to do my part to spread the word.

35

AGING GRACEFULLY?

I was twenty-two years old when I joined the cast of *Y and R*. Today I am sixty-four. I have always been upfront about how old I am. It's a good thing, too, given that my age is easily accessible information via the internet. So you might as well hear it from me!

Aging on television isn't for babies. But it does seem to happen more gradually on a daily broadcast. *Y and R* may have naturally incorporated my pregnancies into their storylines, but growing older wasn't so simple. It can be a very challenging situation. I think with most people, aging isn't something you constantly observe or even think about. I know I didn't. But actors have a unique vehicle for evidence of getting older, with constant reminders that they are looking quite different.

Let's be real, it's just not the same for men. Men get a bit of gray in their hair and wrinkles around their eyes and suddenly they are ready to fill the role of the sexy, silver fox! A woman with gray hair and wrinkles around the eyes? Maybe a . . . grandma? So imagine the pressure actresses feel to present themselves as unrealistically, eternally beautiful.

All this said, actors often resort to fillers and plastic surgery to achieve a look they feel comfortable with. Once they start to notice the small differences in their face, they often decide to take matters into the hands of a plastic surgeon.

Now as I type these words, please know that I have never felt this way. I remember always saying that I looked forward to playing a grandma when I got older. That I was in this business for the long haul, not just to play the vixen! And I would say that I am now past even the *aging* vixen stage! But Grandma? Yes, Nikki is. Several times over! No Botox, filler, or anything with a needle has ever made its way onto my face. And I've received such lovely messages from female fans who profusely thank me for it. It means a lot to them that I have chosen to be candid and unfiltered. They call me brave. Especially because Nikki has quite a few storylines in which, for various reasons, I have chosen to play her with no hair or makeup.

For me, it's not about bravery. It's just making a choice to be true to the scene. But lately I've been watching episodes of *Y and R* and if the camera is on my profile and I have to look down, I'm now seeing this three-chin situation going on. Don't hate me for saying this, but I can't be true to any scene with three chins! I have deemed it to be unacceptable! That being said, I'm taking this opportunity to admit that I've decided to do something about it. This December, I'm going to have a neck lift. (When this reaches your hands, though, December will have long passed. It will be interesting to know how this has all turned out.)

Don't gasp. It's not because I want to look young again. I think the "looking young" ship has long sailed away. I'm perfectly happy to wave goodbye to it. This is something I'm doing for myself. The reason I chose December as the month is because it's the only time out of the year in which I would have time off to heal. A lot of actresses in my line of work, *every* Christmas, they're doing something. Little nips and tucks here and there. I have no judgment.

One of our actresses actually said out loud, years ago, when someone was talking about Christmas break, "Christmas break? Well, isn't that what Christmas break *is for*? To go see your plastic surgeon?" We all laughed, as did she, because she has always been candid about such things.

There could be a huge backlash. I could hear back from people saying *ugh, we've looked up to you, and you sold out.* To that, I say this: Just as it's my right to do what I will with my body, I accept that people are certainly entitled to express their opinions. So say what you will. It won't change anything, though. I do hope my fans understand that I'm not succumbing to any sort of pressure. The show isn't *making* me do it. It's for me.

I encourage women to follow their path to what makes them feel beautiful. Whether it's by changing your diet or doing yoga or getting facials or purchasing hair or, yes, even plastic surgery. At the end of the day, I say do what makes you feel good. You're the *only* one who has to live in the skin you're in. And that's something I've learned to do over the years, in many ways. And I've been able to grow with that love. After the complexities of my tumultuous childhood and young adulthood, I've learned to love the skin I'm in.

And to be very frank, these three chins are very reminiscent of my mother's profile.

And *there* it is . . .

36

BECOMING NIKKI & ENJOYING MEL

People ask me so often, "What's it been like working on a soap?" I never mean to be nonchalant or to throw out replies like, "I dunno. It's just normal days at work for me," but it really is! Forty years of driving to CBS to play Nikki is my normal. Though, don't get me wrong, working on a daytime soap can be quite strenuous. We are one of only a few shows on the air with year-round shooting schedules. Sure, our individual shooting schedules do vary from week to week depending on how many episodes we will be featured in, but a year-round shooting schedule is tough. We are a rare breed of actors, providing *daily* episodes over years and years.

To be specific about how it's done, we get our scripts a week in advance. But oftentimes dialogue can change, even on the day of shooting. So we have to be ready and willing to switch directions and memorize new dialogue at the drop of a hat. Dialogue can be problematic on a show like ours. Actors have been known to struggle with the massive amounts of dialogue we're required to memorize. When you're shooting multiple episodes in a week, that puts a lot of pressure on those with tons of dialogue.

I've seen actors new to the show who come in and you can sense that they have no idea what they're getting themselves into. We have about fifty times more dialogue than a primetime show does. For example, on your typical nighttime drama, maybe they shoot three to ten pages a day on one episode. We're shooting eighty. Eighty pages a day! You have to be able to know what you're getting into or, sadly, you're not going to make it.

If dialogue isn't your cup of tea, you'll spend all of your time on a soap laboring over trying to learn the words. That tension is easy to read on camera. This is sometimes when actors get replaced. And I've seen that happen many times. Sometimes it's like a baptism by fire—you have to be off and running or you'll never make it.

For me, it's not just a medium that depends on having a good memory; it also depends on truly connecting to the character. Once that happens, the lines stay planted in your brain. It's like a muscle that gets strengthened over time. And I've been fortunate to have had decades to connect to Nikki.

How do I connect? I learn from her. In fact, I relate to her on a deep level. For me, Nikki's struggles symbolize perseverance and resilience, and those qualities mirror my own life. What I've had to overcome and sift through hasn't defeated me. Same with Nikki. She serves to remind me of how little we sometimes control in our lives. But instead of succumbing to the madness and being over-whelmed or even feeling victimized, we take faith that our struggles have a deeper meaning. That perhaps we are on a journey, and that in the end things could work out in our favor. Maybe it's important to look back and see the value of the trials we've endured. Those twists and turns, those events—they were the paths laid out to help us to reach our goals. They led us to our destiny. They've certainly led me to mine. Because becoming Nikki changed *everything* for me.

Before I joined the cast of *Y and R* I was drifting from one job to the next. Spending my days driving around Los Angeles, going from audition to audition. Don't get me wrong, I wasn't complaining. An actor's life can be very exciting. But so much gets left undetermined when you live like that. You essentially aren't in control. One moment you're living in L.A., the next you're on a flight and staying for months on location anywhere in the world, living out of a suitcase. Then you're back home and out of work again, literally standing in line at the unemployment office (back then we had lines).

Becoming Nikki eliminated all of that. It gave *me* control. Not to mention I was suddenly thrust into an income bracket I had never known before. A weekly salary? Such stability was intoxicating. I loved it. It was security. Many actors have put in years of hard work and they deserve job security, but very few get to enjoy the fruits of their labor in such a way. Job security is a rare commodity in this industry.

Of course after a while, you get used to the new life that job security affords you. You're wearing better clothes. Driving better cars. Dare I say it—you're no longer earning a living but making a *life*.

Were it not for meeting Carlos Yeaggy on the set of *Y and R*, I would never have given birth to Alex. Were it not for Edward Scott, Lizzie would not be here. Grandkids, too. It's been a domino effect of goodness. And not only did I get to experience being a wife and mother, the show presented it on a silver platter (not a silver bowl!). What actor would ever expect such things like a nursery in your dressing room? Pregnancies written into the scripts?

Were it not for Diane Davis, I would not have joined the cast in the first place. I owe her so much. I am so grateful for the relationship we've had over our lifetimes together. And Bill Bell. He watched a tape and saw Nikki in *me*—he saw my character, my personality, my potential. And I'm so grateful for his enduring faith in me.

Of course, I could spend this entire book talking about things that happened on *Y and R* and things that happened in my life, but that would miss the root of what I've experienced. Because the essential part of life is not about the things you do so much as the people you meet. And in my time on this show, and in this industry, I've met some amazing people. People like my husband, Edward, who I never expected to love as much as I do. Like Eric Braeden, the best acting partner of all time, and my on-screen husband of so many years. People like Bill and Lee Bell, and Carlos, and Lefty, Diane's late husband.

You can't talk about *Y and R* without talking about Bill and Lee Bell. Together, they created and wrote the series. Bill was absolutely larger than life, and in this medium, he was a god. Way back when I was auditioning, I knew that they were the creators, that they'd be watching my footage from Chicago and making the final call. Back then, with them living so far away, I didn't think they'd have such an impact on my life—but wow, was I wrong! I met them in person a month after I was first brought on, at the annual *Y and R* anniversary party, held at The Beverly Hills Hotel. I still remember the green dress that I wore. I was somewhat nervous, since I hadn't been on the show very long and I wasn't yet very close with any of the cast and crew. I had Roberta Leighton and Wings Hauser and a few others, but otherwise, I was still meeting people.

Well, Bill didn't waste any time. He came right up to me and asked me to dance with this peculiar, dreamy look in his eye. Like, a "this can't be real" look. It was a little uncomfortable, as I'd just met him, and his wife was standing right there, but I didn't yet understand that this was just how he was.

Another thing I remember? He called me Nikki! Not Melody!

We finished our dance, and he looked at me for another moment, and he just said, "Captivating. Simply captivating."

At the time, it seemed odd to me, but as I got to know him better, I looked back at that dance and thought, *Oh, that was so Bill. That was Bill Bell.*

Bill was one of those rare talents who didn't just write from nine to five. He inhabited his stories every moment of the day. He was always half there, half not—always in and out of the present. He had that whole cast of characters going in his head 24/7. It's a miracle he kept it all straight, really. If you went to dinner with him, you could just see it in his eyes: he was there most of the time, but sometimes he'd look away, lost in thought. It wasn't that he was distracted, but you knew he was thinking of next month's story. It was concurrent with his real life. And when you look back at all the stories he created—hundreds, if not thousands—it's not hard to recognize his brilliance as a writer.

We lost Bill in April of 2005. Due to complications from Alzheimer's, he had stepped down a few years earlier. That was difficult for us emotionally. However, him leaving this earth was utterly *devastating*. There will never be another like him. Professionally, he breathed life into Nikki and hundreds of others. Personally, he was my dear friend. What a privilege it was to work with one of the greatest visionaries of daytime television.

Another thing I truly appreciate about my time with *Y and R* is that it has allowed and afforded me the opportunity to travel. I have traveled much of the world and in that, gained such an appreciation for other cultures. I truly believe that traveling and education are key to raising well-rounded children. That's another thing I can thank *Y and R* for.

My children have traveled quite a bit as well. Edward and I gifted each child a trip to Europe after they graduated high school with one friend as company. Our expense. They came back like different people. There's nothing like travel to broaden one's perspective, to see how others live and think. You gain such an appreciation for other cultures as well as your own. It's a beautiful, humbling thing. Travel is a certain type of education that you simply can't get in a classroom, no matter how great the school is. The world is the best classroom of all.

In addition, *Y and R* has afforded me all the creature comforts of home. And by creature comforts, I mean actual creatures! So many animals: cats, dogs, endless fish, a bunny, even hermit crabs. Many pets have lived (and still do!) in our home. Some of those animals have traveled to live with our adult children, like Lizzie's beloved dachshund. I must share how Luca came to live with us.

Lizzie was a very well-behaved child. Sweet-natured, obedient, and calm. Even as an infant, she rarely cried. She was sleeping though the night at five weeks old. Elizabeth pretty much went along with whatever Mommy said. She didn't ask questions, didn't put up a fight. Some parents might call her the perfect child as far as behavior goes. I know I did! As she grew older, she was always the teacher's pet. Her teachers would rave about how amazing she was in class. Her report cards typically labeled her as a star student. She was that child who rarely did anything wrong. She was also such a Mommy's girl. We still tease her to this day because when she was small, if family members or friends offered to do something like say, tie her shoe, she would scowl at them and very politely reply, "Mommy will do it."

I used to call her my serious child because she was always so obedient and *serious*. I remember once when my dear friend, Catherine Hickland, was chatting with Liz in our kitchen, and exclaimed, "Oh, Lizzie. You're just the cutest little squirrel!"

My serious four-year-old replied, "I am not a squirrel. And I do not wish to be a squirrel."

We bring that up every now and then.

"Oh, Lizzie." I'll tease. "Remember when you did not wish to be a squirrel?"

Anyway, when Liz was a teenager we had just lost our beloved Springer Spaniel, Cassie, and for the first time in years there was no dog in the house. Liz, in the meantime, had become enamored with dachshunds and wanted one more than anything. She was adamant that she go out and purchase the dog herself with her allowance money. All on her own. I was fine with this. But I did have a few rules.

1. The dog must be female.
2. The dog must also be a rescue.
3. Absolutely NO puppies. Too much work!

I didn't know it yet, but she and Alex were in cahoots. They left the house one Saturday morning and came home with:

1. A brand new puppy!
2. Not a rescue.
3. A male!

It's one of the only times I can remember Liz not listening to me. I had given her three rules and she broke them all! But this little puppy was literally riding in her pocket. What could I do? She named him Luca and there he pretty much stayed. In her pocket. They were so close, those two. And even though I was not happy about what she'd done, everyone fell in love with Luca once he was in the house. She knew this would happen!

Luca is still enjoying life with his mistress. Dachshunds have one of the longest average life spans of any breed! We ended up adding our gregarious Lola, a fellow dachshund, to the mix later. They are absolutely devoted to one another, and both are still going strong. They live with Lizzie and her family.

There was one other time Lizzie sort of went rogue, if you will, and broke from her perfect child syndrome. One day when she was around five years old, we couldn't find her in the house. We searched and searched and were starting to panic. *God, where was she?* Eventually we did find her—under the desk cabinet, in the kitchen. She had been hiding under there hoping to be out of sight, with *scissors*.

And yep, you guessed it, she'd decided to cut her own hair. Though they were children's scissors, they could still cut hair splendidly. Oh my goodness, it was not an attractive outcome. What a zig-zag mess she had made.

"Why did you do this?" I asked, seeing the piles of blonde locks lying beside her.

"Well," she declared innocently, "because Jennifer just cut her hair."

I sighed. She wanted to look like her older sister. Maybe another mom may have gotten upset but based on all I went through as a child, Lizzie's terrible haircut was truly no big deal. We took her to a hairstylist later that week to get it all straightened out, and it wasn't long before it grew back.

Speaking of Jennifer, she was another near-perfect child. As it happens, she and I share very similar features, which have convinced strangers that she is my biological daughter. We have had a lot of fun with that! (All I can say is that my husband knows what he likes!) She was a great student, had tons of friends, and was one of her school's tennis champions. She has always been an avid animal lover and today treats her enormous dogs as family members.

Fiercely devoted to our family unit, Edward and I can always count on her to drop everything, if need be, and help with any unexpected development for the good of the family. Her nine-year-old twins, our first grandchildren, are a joy to behold. Watching them become their own unique individuals has filled us with pride and wonder.

One of our proudest days was when she married her John at their fairytale wedding in 2007. What an elegant, beautiful, and poised bride she was. Not at all nervous, and thrilled to be marrying her soulmate, she seemed to channel a regal Grace Kelly. Many guests who attended still gush about her wedding to us all these years later.

My girls and I have such a wonderful relationship. And I so enjoy watching them with *their* children. They are *wonderful* mothers. I couldn't be more proud of them. Lizzie really was born to be a mother. She's so good with her two angels. And of course, Alex is amazing with her precocious three-year-old.

Though he was perfectly healthy in every way, Alex introduced American Sign Language as an additional way to communicate when he was an infant. Sign language for babies was something Alex had learned of and felt that she had the patience to do. I really think other mothers should consider it. It was a ton of work but because of ASL, he was potty-trained at eight months and communicating before he could speak. An incredible thing to witness. He recently had his first parent-teacher conference and they couldn't say enough amazing things about him! *So* bright and . . . communicative.

Needless to say, I am a very proud Grandma and Mom. It's been wonderful to spend my life with them. And I do enjoy fawning over their mothering skills. It seems to come naturally to them.

In addition to ASL, my daughter Alex speaks fluent Italian and Spanish. After she graduated from high school, she attended UC Berkeley and majored in Art with a minor in Italian. She then moved to Italy to earn her Masters in fashion design. While there, she also learned the ancient art of hand-sewing *anything* from older local seamstresses, who will seemingly be taking their expertise and secrets to the grave with them. But she wanted to be a part of the generation that was making sure their expertise lives on. Alex is so gifted as a seamstress—she can do what many others can't just because she took the time to learn the craft outside of her native country. Today she is a very talented fashion designer.

She's lived in Siena and Milan. She's also lived in Sicily, and for the last part of her years in Italy she lived in Rome. Alex speaks Italian so well that natives think they recognize her Roman accent!

"You must be from Rome!" they exclaim.

But no. Alex is from Los Angeles!

I'm not quite as impressive; I can speak some French (though sadly I've forgotten so much), as well as Spanish. Learning new languages expands the mind. Though it's for practical, geographical reasons, I love that European countries put such a strong emphasis on learning other languages. I wish that we did this in the United States.

Now don't go thinking that my life is perfect! Even though I've shot more than 5,000 episodes of *The Young and the Restless* at this point, I still do the same boring things I've always done! Confession: I didn't learn French in *France*. No, I learned it by listening to French CDs on my then-long commute in L.A. traffic to and from work.

It's true that *Y and R* made my life easier, but it hasn't changed the core of who I am. I still play Sudoku every morning followed by the crossword. I'm still a voracious reader. I still *love* Lucy, still watch it (though at this point, I know all of the dialogue from every episode by heart!). I still prefer comedies and watch them on TV when I can. I still love my animals, like my baby girl, Reilly. I must tell the story of how she came into my life.

A few years ago, Edward went to the South-Central Animal Shelter to scout locations for a remote sequence for *The Bold and the Beautiful*. He went on a Saturday by himself, and before driving down again the next day, he asked me to come along for the ride.

"No thanks," I remember saying. "Safe driving. See you when you get back."

"But I saw a dog there that I think you might want to see."

A dog? For me? I perked up. Our doxies had recently gone to live with Lizzie and he knew I was heartsick at no longer having a pup in the house. I hopped in the car.

When we arrived, we learned that the dog he'd had his eye on was no longer available. So we walked up and down the aisles, perusing all the poor babies that were unlucky enough to be caged there. At one point, Edward and I went in separate directions. Shortly after, I came upon this furless, skin-and-bone little thing sharing her living quarters with two other dogs that were much larger than she was. The moment our eyes met, we began an "eye conversation" that has yet to stop!

She followed me with her eyes wherever I went. I talked to her through the cage and she seemed to understand everything I said to her. As this was going on, an employee came up and asked if there was any dog I would like to take out of the cage to get to know better. Of course I pointed to the sad little dog that appeared to be on her last legs. I asked the employee what breed the dog was. She wasn't sure but thought perhaps she could be a Chinese Crested, as they are naturally very slim and hairless, except for a little tuft on the top of their head. She picked her up and placed her in my arms, directing me to a private, grassy area where prospective adoptive parents can get acquainted with their possible adoptees. As I walked towards the yard's bench, her eyes were pleading, *"Please, please take me home with you! I'll be a good girl and won't be any trouble."*

I tried to put her down on the grass so that we could play but she wouldn't let go of my arms. It was like holding a monkey! We "talked" for quite a while, all the time with her in my arms. Edward came along at this point and wondered what I was doing with "that pathetic little dog!" He had arrived too late! I had already decided that this sweet, I-don't-even-know-what-breed-this-dog-is pooch was mine. We were meant to be together. Fated, some would say.

As it turned out, she wasn't a Chinese Crested. She was a mixed terrier in such dire shape that she had lost all her hair and was reduced to skin and bone. When I took her to her first vet appointment, he told me that stress can cause a dog to lose their hair. I could only imagine the terrible life she'd led before. He assured me that with a little love and regular feedings, she would grow her hair back and fill out. He was absolutely right!

From that first moment at the shelter, she has never wavered from being the most loyal dog I have ever had. When I am not at home, she mopes. When I *am* home, she follows me everywhere, by my side or at my feet. She sleeps with me, is fiercely protective of me, and has kept her eye-promise in being the best dog in the world. We adore each other. The day that we found her was St. Patrick's Day. In keeping with our luck of the Irish, we wanted to give her an Irish name. So we named her Reilly.

Rescue pups, *I Love Lucy* reruns, Sudoku . . . my life can be wonderfully simple. I certainly didn't expect things to veer from the strange and unimaginable to something so ideal for me. I went from living a nightmare to a dream. I have *Y and R* to thank for that. My life went from overwhelming, painful, and difficult, to easy, carefree, and happy. Peaceful. *Normal.* Was it karma? Luck? Fate? Maybe destiny.

Yes, I had to move through many metamorphoses, wrong turns, changes of direction, and more, to get here. I may never fully understand the exact particulars of how one thing leads to the next. But I have become quite the staunch fatalist. The one thing I do know with absolute certainty is that I'm not ashamed to admit that I've been very happy in my adult life.

I am happy still.

POSTSCRIPT

A MESSAGE FROM
THE WORD WRANGLER

M el and I share the same literary agent and when he reached out to me about helping her with her book, I was pretty sure she would never go along with it. I remember Googling the name Melody Thomas Scott because it sounded so familiar. I took one look at her and of course I remembered growing up with her on my TV screen as my mom or aunt or older cousins watched their favorite stories.

"Oh, I *know* her!" I declared to my agent, Uwe. "But do you really think she wants *me* helping her with her book?"

At this point in my life I hadn't sold a book yet. I was just starting out my career as a novelist and in my mind, she was daytime TV royalty. Plus, I felt she might be afraid of our cultural differences.

"And does she know I'm black?" I almost whispered.

Uwe laughed. "Mel wouldn't care if you were green. She's looking for a right fit as she has a rather interesting story to tell. I think you two will connect. Why not take a meeting with her and see what happens?"

I agreed but I was beyond nervous. I sent her an email introducing myself and asking where she would like to meet. I imagined she'd choose some posh spot in Beverly Hills. Maybe the Beverly Hills Hotel or some swanky restaurant. I checked my closet to see if I had any nice dresses.

"How about Peet's Coffee on Ventura?" she replied.

Peet's Coffee? I knew the spot. I visited there often. It was right across the street from my accountant's office and near Chipotle. This is where she wanted to meet? At an old coffee shop in one of the busiest sections of Studio City?

"Sounds good!" I replied and I geared up for our meeting. I guessed I wouldn't need a fancy dress after all.

I told my mom who I was meeting. "I may have an opportunity to help Melody Thomas Scott with her memoir."

My mom's eyes almost popped out of her head. "She's Nikki!" my mom squealed. "Oh, tell her I'm a big fan. Tell her I said hi."

The next week I'm sitting at Peet's Coffee and waiting on Melody Thomas Scott and her entourage to arrive. So imagine my surprise when she rushes to my table alone, looking so very normal.

"Hello Melody." I said as professionally as I could. "Pleasure to meet you."

She plopped into the seat across from me. "Oh, call me Mel!" Then she leaned forward. "And have I got a story to tell you!" She smiled. "Are you sure you're ready for this?"

And hour later and we were still chatting and laughing like we'd known one another for decades. Never did she ask my age or what I write or how long I've been writing. She just seemed to . . . trust me. Finally, I had to bring up my fears.

"You'd be okay with *me* helping you?"

She smiled. "Oh, Uwe sent me some of the pages from your book." At this time my debut novel, *Tiffany Sly Lives Here Now*, had not sold, so she'd only read pages from a Word document. "I thought it was brilliant. I think you're absolutely lovely. And I love that you're an actor too."

"I thought me being black might be of concern. I figured you'd want someone from the same cultural background as you. To better understand you."

"I couldn't care less about any of that!" She laughed. "Besides, no one is from the same cultural background as me. I'm from a long line of crazy!" She laughed again. I laughed too. "You seem to get me." She said simply. "And for me it's all about connection. Did Uwe tell you that?"

I nodded. He did in fact tell me that.

"I'm ready to get started." Mel said excitedly. "How *do* we get started?"

I couldn't believe it. This woman who I had grown up watching on television was sitting across from me, treating me as if I were her equal. There was no pretense. No air about her. All I got was warmth, light, love, and acceptance.

We set up a time to begin discussing the particulars of her book. She wanted us to meet at her home, where we would have privacy.

Driving up to Mel's gated community was rather intimidating. I had to stop and check in with security.

"Hello," I said. "I'm here to see Melody Thomas Scott?"

"Oh, you're here to see Mel! You're Dana. She told me all about you," the security guard said.

She did?

"You're on the forever list. Mel said when you come we should treat you well and send you right in."

I grinned. "She did? Oh. Ok."

I was let through and pulled up to Mel's house. Nervously, I rang the doorbell. A dog was barking loudly as Mel swung the door open dressed in pajamas.

"Reilly, be good!" she said to the little white terrier barking at me. "Don't worry about Reilly. She's harmless. You like dogs, right? Because if not I can send her away."

"Oh, I love dogs." And I do. And little Reilly did look quite harm-less. I looked around. The house was so massive and gorgeous. "Should I take off my shoes?" I asked politely.

She shrugged. "Only if you want."

I followed her into the kitchen, where I met her husband. "This is Edward," she said. "Edward's going to give us privacy. So good-bye, Edward."

I shook hands with Edward Scott. He too seemed just about as nice and normal as they come.

"Would you like a drink?" Mel asked. "Or an orange?"

An orange? Nobody had ever offered me an orange before. But she had a giant bowl filled with what looked like freshly picked or-anges. So bright and beautiful. It added a certain light to the room. "Sure. I love oranges." I immediately felt right at home.

That's how it's been ever since. Meeting with Mel at her home, chatting in the backyard. Sometimes eating oranges. We've laughed so much. We've cried too. If we ended up working late, she'd ask if I wanted to stay over in one of their guest rooms.

"Oh, but I have a daughter," I explained.

"A daughter?" she replied. "How lovely. I adore kids. Bring her next time. She can swim in the pool while we talk."

This is just how Mel is. Years later, nothing has changed. She is still the same warm, loving soul who offered me an orange on our first day working together.

I don't think ghostwriter is the right term for what I did with Mel. She very much wrote the words on these pages. I like to say I helped her organize her thoughts—I was her professional word wrangler. She'd write pages and I'd offer my thoughts and edits. The words I wrote were taken right out of her mouth. This is her story. Her words. Her journey.

Mel seems to have been on a quest for normalcy. And that is ex-actly what you get from her. Her house is warm and inviting. Her family couldn't be sweeter, kinder, or more loving. Watching her with her kids would sometimes bring tears to my eyes. To see the love her children have for her . . . there are no words to describe it. In my life, I've never seen children who seem to admire and show such kind regard and respect to their mother. It's a beautiful thing to witness.

There is also an energy about Mel that you have to live to understand and fully appreciate. It becomes a part of you. Mel doesn't know this, but I've had so many miracles come into my life since I started working with her. When we began our professional relationship I was in the depths of despair, battling my daughter's autism, my career in shambles, feeling as if I had nothing and nowhere to turn. Mel became like a mother figure to me. Her acceptance and willingness to give me a chance to help her tell her story helped me to climb out of my dark night and grab on to the light. I am eternally grateful. May the energy of Mel seep through the pages of this book and bless you as much as it has blessed me.

Mel's been looking for normal her whole life. She's definitely earned it.

She's certainly found it.

ACKNOWLEDGMENTS

I can't begin thanking anyone before thanking my incredible collaborator, Dana L. Davis. Her talent and keen ability to help structure my crazy life was invaluable. I don't think she realized what she was getting into when she first signed on to this project! As our many hours of sharing my stories wore on, I expected her to think I was a lost cause. A Hollywood nut! But Dana is an actress herself, inherently aware of what the life of an actor can be. She is now a lifelong friend. I adore her.

My literary agent, Uwe Stender, and his Triada US Literary Agency, were also vital to making this book a reality. With Uwe's tenacity and perseverance, my story found a home after an almost-ten-year effort. His gentle nudging, which grew into major pushing, became the force that I needed. From the first time he listened to some of the tales of my past, sitting on the patio of my home so many years ago, he knew there was a book worth pursuing in me.

I am forever grateful to him and his miracle staff: Laura (Elle) Thompson, one of the best editors and tech support around (which I, the low-tech, novice writer, desperately needed!), who I am deeply indebted to. And Tori Bovalino, another editing and tech whiz, and thankfully a much-needed source of Uwe's moral support!

Thanks to the good people at Diversion Books, who believed in me from the beginning: Scott Waxman; Mark Weinstein, who has such insight and natural inquisitiveness; Melanie Madden, whose kindness and understanding made my job easier; Keith Wallman, a go-getter, whose charm is only outmatched by his intelligence, ensuring success by all; and Emily Hillebrand and Amanda Farbanish.

Thanks to my very patient family: Edward, Jennifer, Alex, and Elizabeth, for their years-long support and encouragement while putting up with me through this healing process. I can never thank you enough. I adore you all.

Thanks to my *Y and R* family, CBS Television, and Sony Pictures Television: our hardworking producing teams, writing teams, directing teams, actors, and crew, from past to present. And so many others of note:

Marla Adams, Robert Adamson, Kay Alden, Ricky Alverez, the late Steve Artmont, Craig Aspden, Susan Banks, Amanda L. Beall, Jeff Beldner, the late Bill Bell, Bill Bell, Jr., Brad Bell, Colleen Bell, Lauralee Bell, Lee Phillip Bell, Maria Arena Bell, Meg Bennett, Peter Bergman, Derek Berlatsky, Marc Beruti, Joe Bevacqua, Sara A. Bibel, Roberto Bosio, Derek Blum, Greg Blum, Robert Bolger, Eric Braeden, Vanessa Bragdon, Tracey Bregman, Fritz Brekeller, John Bromberek, James Harmon Brown, Ed Burgess, Scott Burkhart, Melissa Burton, Sasha Calle, Gail Camacho, Richard Casady, Sharon Case, Tom Casiello, Tricia Cast, RC Cates, Courtney Philbrook Chapman, Daniel Cisneros, Tamara (Dutch) Clatterback, Jessica Collins, Kelsey Collins, the late John Conboy, Michael Conforti, the late Jeanne Cooper, the late Jim Crosby, the late Willie Dahl,

Michael Damian, Doug Davidson, Eileen Davidson, Stan Dembecki, Patti Denney, Mike Denney, Don Diamont, Mike Dobson, Sean Dominic, Jerry Douglas, Amy Dunn, Christopher Dunn, Missy Egan, Michael Eilbaum, Joan Ellsworth, Sara Endsley, John Enos, Janice Ferri Esser, the late Michael Evans, Kimberly Everett, Cait Fairbanks, John Fisher, Steven Ford, Genie Francis, Jimmy Freeman, Marisa Garcia, Ralph Gertel, the late Luis Godinez, Chico Godinez, Barry Grant, Michael Graziadei, the late Paul Greiner, Josh Griffith, Camryn Grimes, Mark Grossman, Bob Guzzi, Andrew Hachem, David Hasselhoff, Wings Hauser, Jen Haybach, the late Eddie Heim, Amelia Heinle, Elizabeth Hendrickson, Brendan Higgins, Heather Hill, Randy Hill, the late Harry Hirsch, David Hoffman, Randy Holland, Juliette Huerta, Russ Hurley, Sean Isom, Bryton James, the late Scha Jani, Alex Jenson, Andrea Joel, Dean Johnson, Lucy Johnson, Tyler Johnson, Kathy Jones, Sean Kanan, Matt Kane, the late Wes Kenney, Steve Kent, Christel Khalil, Christina Knack, Kai Kim, Hunter King, Dean Lamont, Mark Landon, Brandon Lankford, the late Russell Latham, Joe Lawrence, Morgan Lawrence, Tracy Lawrence, Tristan Lake Leabu, Christian LeBlanc, Elizabeth LeBrun, Roberta Leighton, Alyvia Alyn Lind, Kate Linder, Jeff Long, William Looper, Tony Lorito, Adriana Lucio, Thad Luckinbill, Tom Luth, Beth Maitland, Pete Mallard, Matt Marchant, Lynn Martin. Marlene Mason, Noel Maxam, Elliott Mayhew, the late Dorothy McGuire, Julianna McCarthy, John McCook, Tom McDermott, Sally McDonald, the late Brian McManus, Michael Mealor, Mondee Megas, Anne Mendelson, Lauren Mendoza, Justine Mercado, Erica Meyer, Steve Milberger, Andreea Moldovan, Mark Mooney, the late Shel Mooney, Shemar Moore, Mishael Morgan, Tony Morino, Nancy Morrison, Joshua Morrow, Conal O'Brien, Josh O'Connell, John O'Hurley, Matt Olsen, Melissa Ordway, Nancy Ortenberg, the late Frank Pacelli, Bob Parucha, J. Eddie Peck, Tommy Persson, Jill Farren Phelps, Robbin Phillips, Tommy Puckett, Greg Rikaart, the late

Paul Rauch, Quinn Redeker, Scott Reeves, Owen Renfroe, Bill Roberts, Regina Rodriguez, Alex Romero, Larry Roslaw, Matt Rusher, Cameron Saenz, Nick Saenz, Greg Salmon, Brytni Sarpy, Jennifer Savala, Greg Savalas, Laura Schaffer, Nick Schillace, Anne Schoettle, Keven Scotti, Ashleigh Sigal, Jack Smith, Sean Smith, the late Kristoff St. John, Natalie Minardi Slater, Ben Spaulding, Dorchelle Stafford, Michelle Stafford, Denise Palm Stones, Sally Sussman, Raquel Tarbet, Kayla Taylor, Gabriella Alaimo Thomas, Jason Thompson, Laura Tiefer, Gina Tognoni, Heather Tom, Lou Trabbie, Stefan Tsarofski, Paul Tulley, Jordi Vilasuso, Renee Villafan, Margot Wain, Bonnie Walker, Pat Walker, Laura Walsh, Jess Walton, Andrzej Warzocha, Kay Wataguchi, Herbie Weaver, Patty Weaver, Jimmy Weems, Maura West, Jacqueline Wickert, Alvin Williams, Tonya Lee Williams, Steven Williford, Lynn Wood, Lauren Woodland, Renee Young, Jackie Zavala, Teresa Zimmerman, and David Zyla. The list could go on . . .

Thanks to our millions of *Y and R* fans all over the world—without whom we would not be the enduring force that so many have enjoyed for the last forty-seven years. Your staunch loyalty and support mean more to me than I can say. Thank you for always having my back:

Jessica Aufiero, Margie Collazo, Sylvana Daher, Wendy Davies, Leslie Williams Davis, Heather Freedman, Erianna Hall, Matt Hanvey, Cathy Keever, Chris Korman, Marlene Langois, Navell Lee (Buzz Buzzworthy), Marie-Michelle Marier, Marianne Michotte, Kyla Miller, Lucindia Osbourn, Marina Papthemistokleous, Kate Kubsch Roberts, Dan Saunders, Frank Sette, Michael Sette, Joe and Mary Sieber, Amal Smejkal, Amanda Smith, Angelina Solis, Leigh Daisy Williams, Donna Woods, Cece Zammit, and literally millions more . . .

Thank you to the press outlets, journalists, photographers, and publicity wizards who have always treated me with such kindness and respect over the years. Yours is a thankless job, but you are our secret weapon in navigating this business. Please accept my heartfelt praise and gratitude:

Anne-Marie Allocca, Eva Basler, Meredith Berlin, Monty Brinton, Elise Bromberg, Melissa Burton, Beverly Byrd, Roberta Caploe, Alan Carter, Francis Cavanaugh, Amanda Champagne, Janet DiLauro, Chris Ender, Sue Facter, Michael Fairman, Sonja Flemming, Jeremy Fraser, Phil Gonzales, Candy Havens, Carolyn Hinsey, Linda Hirsch, Kathy Hutchins, David Johnson, Matt Kane, Roger Karnbad, Cliff Lipson, Lynn Leahey, Michael Logan, Michael Maloney, Ed Mann, Julie McElwain, Aaron Montgomery, Ruby Montgomery, Geraldine Overton, Dawn Owens, Devin Owens, John Paschal, Connie Passalacqua, Nancy Reichardt, Damon Romine, Tina Rosener, Rosemary Rossi, Robert Rourke, Angela Shapiro, Libby Slate, Stephanie Sloane, Lillian B. Smith, Sean Smith, Richard Spencer, Tom Stacy, Sheila Steinbach, Olivia Stren, Linda Sussman, Kathleen Tanji, Frank Tobin, Mimi Torchin, Gabrielle Winkel, Howard Wise, Renee Young, and so many others.

We all have those special friends whose loyalty, sense of humor, encouragement, and generosity of spirit make everything all the more worthwhile. I am blessed to have so many. Here are just a few:

Claudine Battisti, Joe Bevacqua, Robert Bolger, Lyn Bowler, Brendan Burns, Bob Caudle, Bonnie Caudle, Wanda Clark, the late Van Cliburn, Vinny Colon, the late Ray Combs, Jez Davidson, the late Julian Davis, Patti Denney, the late Julie Even, Randy Even, Karen Faye, Nathalie Fino, Jimmy Freeman, Amelia Heinle, Catherine Hickland, Gayle Jacobs, Jennifer Johns, Melina Kanakaredes, Matt Kane, Kenn Kastle, Lou and Melissa Klein, Chris Korman, the late Russell Latham, Roberta Leighton, Tony Lorito, Noel Maxam, David Michaels, Andreea Moldovan, Glenna Norris, Lilana Novakovich, the late Frank Pacelli, Neal Pargman, Suzie and Tommy Persson,

ACKNOWLEDGMENTS

Traci Pontello, Linda Riha, Salila Sharma, Anne Schoettle, Frank Tobin, Cathy Tomas, Kristi Trimble, Carol Whelan-Garrett, Bonnie Walker, Pat Walsh, Alvin Williams, Stefana Williams, the late Jenna Wittman, Ric Wyman, the late Carlos Yeaggy, the late Greg York, and the late David Zimmerman . . .

Thanks to Suzie and Lorena.

And, of course, my sweet Reilly.

I've also been so fortunate to have the assistance of some pretty terrific Career Influencers, including:

Susan Banks, Courtney Barnes, Charles Bush, Diane Davis, Michael Einfeld, Alan Ellsweig, the late Jonathan Exley, Brenda Feldman, Tom Langan, Michael Logan, Bob Olive, John Paschal, Andi Schechter, Frank Tobin, and Cathy Tomas.

Lastly, but certainly foremost in an actor's world . . . The Glam Squad:

Thanks to Bernie Ardia, the late Steve Artmont, Justine Beech, Robert Bolger, Scott Burkhart, Patti Denney, Karen Faye, Cary Fetman, the late Bruce Wayne Fischer, Kevan Hall, Elif Inanc, Bernard Jacobs, Jennifer Johns, Jeff Jones, the late Russell Latham, Romaine Markus, Nancy Morrison, Regina Rodriguez, Dorchelle Stafford, Maurice Tannenbaum, Bonnie Walker, the late Jenna Wittman, Alexandra Yeaggy, the late Greg York, Jackie Zavala, and David Zyla.

If some names have been repeated in different categories, they deserve to be.

I'll leave you with Bill Bell's famous, forever-accurate words, to which we all still try to strive: "Conflict is the essence of drama."

INDEX

ABOUT THE AUTHOR

MELODY THOMAS SCOTT is best known for her Emmy-nominated work in the iconic role of Nikki Reed Newman, a character she's played for forty years and counting on America's number-one day-time television drama *The Young and the Restless*. She's also appeared in feature films with the likes of Clint Eastwood and John Wayne, and worked with esteemed directors like Alfred Hitchcock and Brian De Palma. Melody is known for her charitable efforts with ATAS Television Cares and the Save the Earth Foundation. She lives with her husband, Edward Scott, and beloved rescue terrier, Reilly, in Beverly Hills, California.

Original Al Hirschfeld portrait that Edward
commissioned for my 25th *Y&R* anniversary, 2004